Uncle John Carr

Portrait of John Carr, 1785. *City of York Council (Mansion House)*

Uncle John Carr

The Diaries of his Great-nieces,
Harriet and Amelia Clark

Transcribed and edited by Corita Myerscough for the
York Georgian Society's Millennium Project

Best wishes
Corita Myerscough

ISBN 0 950 3663 58

Published by
York Georgian Society
Registered Charity No 233175

Designed, printed and distributed by
Maxiprint Designers & Colour Printers
Kettlestring Lane, Clifton Moor,
York YO30 4XF England
Telephone: 01904 692000
www.maxiprint.co.uk

Uncle John Carr

The Diaries of his Great Nieces,
Harriet and Amelia Clark

Contents

Uncle John Carr

List of Illustrations

Harriet's Diary for 1795

Wentworth Woodhouse - Engraved by J. Shury from a drawing by Nathaniel Whittock (c. 1828-1831), belonging to the editor.

Farnley Hall - facing page 81 in J. Wheater's *Some Historic Mansions of Yorkshire,* (Leeds, Richard Jackson, 1888). YML. Y/LB 8.8 WHE Reproduced by kind permission of the Dean and Chapter of York.

Rydal Waterfall and Bridge - An engraving from the Minster Library's Collection of Topographical Prints, XR2/1, dated 1817.
Reproduced by kind permission of the Dean and Chapter of York.

Hamilton Palace - An engraving signed 'Storer & Greig sculp'. London. Publish'd by Vernon, Hood & Sharpe, Poultry, Novr. 1st 1807. Facing p. 160 in Vol. III, *The Beauties of Scotland.* (Edinburgh, Arch, Constable & Co. & John Brown, 1806.)

Royal Bank of Scotland, Edinburgh - Signed 'E. Mitchell, Sculpt., this engraving was published by Vernon & Good in February 1805. Facing p. 89 in Vol. I, *Beauties of Scotland,* (Edinburgh, Thomson, Bonar & John Brown, 1805.)

Register Office, Edinburgh - An engraving by R. Scott and drawn by A. Carse, appearing opposite p. 140 also in Vol. 1, *Beauties of Scotland* and published in London by Vernon & Good in February 1805.
These three Scottish engravings appear by courtesy of Mr. Darrell Buttery.

Sedbury Park, near Gilling - An engraving from the Minster Library's Collection of Topographic Prints (Yorkshire), April 1790. S112.
Reproduced by kind permission of the Dean and Chapter of York.

Amelia's Diary for 1796

St. Peter's Church, Horbury. Engraved by T. Malton.
Reproduced by kind permission of Dr. Terry Friedman.
Hack Fall, Grewelthorpe - An engraving by J. Rogers, SC, from a drawing by N. Whittock, c. 1828-1832, in the possession of the York Georgian Society.

Rutherford Bridge - Reproduced from a drawing in John Carr's *Bridge Book of the North Riding* by kind permission of the County Record Office, North Yorkshire County Council, Northallerton.

Buxton - A panoramic view, from a drawing by E. Dayes, facing p. 441 Vol. III, *The Beauties of England and Wales* by I. Britton & E. W. Braylay, (London, Thomas Maiden, 1802-4.)
Reproduced by kind permission of the Dean and Chapter of York.

Basildon - The Principal Front of Basildon House, in Berkshire, the Seat of Sir Francis Sykes, Bart. London, April 15, 1797. Engraved and published by George Richardson.
Reproduced by courtesy of Reading Local Studies Library.

Basildon Park, Berkshire - Plate 60, engraved by Walker, from an original drawing by Dayes. Published July 1st, 1794 by Harrison & Co., No. 18 Paternoster Row, London.
Reproduced by courtesy of Reading Local Studies Library.

Newark Town Hall - Engraving facing page 385 in *Annals of Nottinghamshire - History of the County of Nottingham, including the borough* by Thomas Bailey, (Nottingham, Simpkin, Marshall & Co., c. 1853.)

Amelia's Diary for 1798

Old House in Watergate Street, Chester - with the inscription Gods Providence is Mine Inheritance (1652). Published by T. Catherall, Chester.

A Mill on the Llanberris side of Snowdon - An engraving from an original painting by C. Marshall, belonging to the editor.

Tabley House - Published by courtesy of the University of Manchester, Tabley House Collection. From the Devis painting of the south front. Photograph: Photographic Survey - Courtauld Institute of Art.

Acknowledgements

The York Georgian Society is indebted to the Dean and Chapter of York by whose kind permission these Diaries have been reproduced for publication to commemorate the Millennium. Some of the illustrations have also been taken from books and engravings housed in the Minster Library, and again are reproduced by kind permission of the Dean and Chapter.

The Editor would like to thank the members of the Society who have been so supportive, particularly those who have given advice and encouragement, provided books of reference and some of the engravings used; they include Dr Terry Friedman, Dr Ivan Hall, Professor E. Youngson, Messrs Michael Brown, Darrell Buttery, Roger Carr-Whitworth, Bob Hale, David Harrison and Ian Macvean. The staffs of the Minster Library, Dringhouses Library, and the Local History Section of York Central Library have been most generous with their help. The Archivists of the Record Offices of Lancaster and of North Yorkshire, the Local Studies Librarians at Birmingham, Gloucester, Newark and Reading and the Archivist of Tabley House have been unstinting in providing valuable assistance as have the Courtauld Institute and York City Art Gallery.

Thanks are also due to Miss Glenys Morris for sharing her local knowledge, much needed for transcribing Amelia's Journal of the Tour of North Wales, to Mrs Rosita Whittall for checking the typescript, and to Ms Carrie Geddes of Maxiprint for her publishing knowhow.

If anyone has been forgotten, please forgive the omission; the involvement of so many people has enabled the appearance of this publication.

Introduction

The three journals transcribed in this volume are the diaries of Harriet and Amelia Clark, two of John Carr's great-nieces. They were the daughters of Thomas Clark of Bankside House, Thorne, near Doncaster, and his wife Ann Carr, eldest daughter of John Carr's brother, Robert. The girls were the second and third daughters in a family of 4 daughters and 6 sons, Harriet being born in October 1776 and Amelia on 20th August 1778, so nineteen and sixteen when they set out on their 1795 adventure with their Uncle.

In 1986 their diaries were bought by the York Civic Trust and presented to the Dean and Chapter, to be housed in the Minster Library; until then the three slim copy books had been in the keeping of the the the late Col. R.G. Parker of Browsholme Hall, whose ancestor, Thomas Goulbourne Parker, married Mary Ann Carr of Carr Lodge, Horbury, a great-great-niece of John Carr. While they have been mentioned by Colvin[1] and Giles Worsley,[2] as far as is known, they have not appeared in print before.

The first diary was written by Harriet, entitled *Harriet Clark's Journal of the Tour made in the year 1795*, and covers the period from 2nd June to 16th December. The second volume, *Miss Clark's Journal, made in the year 1795*, commences on 17th August 1795 and finishes at the beginning of October and repeats, almost word for word, the text of the first journal. This has not, therefore, been included. The writing of both girls is so similar that it is virtually impossible to tell who was penning each diary, but it is presumed that this second volume was written by Amelia, who only undertook part of the tour. The third book contains *Amelia Clark's Journal of the Tour made in the year 1796* and *Amelia Clark's Journal through North Wales from Thorp Arch made in the year 1798*.

Editorially as little alteration as possible has been made in order that the diaries retain their individuality; there are turns of phrase, such as 'in our way', which both girls employ. Repeated anecdotes and measurements and details of buildings which appear for a second time have been edited out. They also use idiosyncratic punctuation, so full-stops have been inserted where necessary to replace the semi-colons they invariably use throughout the text. Capital letters are often missing and apart from inserting them at the beginning of sentences, their omission has been retained. The spelling, both of words and place names, which had not as then been standardized, has been left untouched unless the meaning of the text is opaque; this was the case in Amelia's journal covering the journey to North Wales, when she used a 'K', which does not occur in the Welsh alphabet, in place of a 'C'. The marginal notes made by the sisters have been placed within square brackets [ ] within the text, while words omitted appear in round brackets ( ).

Wherever possible, footnotes provide additional information, but not all the people mentioned have been traced, nor all the properties. Harriet makes allusions to John Carr's involvement in buildings which, to date, have not been substantiated - Sir Lawrence Dundas's house in Edinburgh and the Piece Hall in Halifax, while details of, for example, luggage, laundry, accommodation and transport are sketchy, and one longs to know more! That they travelled both on horseback and by phaeton is confirmed in a later, unpublished diary written by Miss Elizabeth Chivers who, aged 21, accompanied the Heaton sisters and Carr on his last journey in 1805.[3] Then they covered almost nine hundred miles safely "with either the Carriages or Horses," Carr driving "a pair of spirity little horses in his Phaeton." In 1795 he and his great-niece, Harriet, were travelling for "one hundred and ninety nine days", with Amelia joining them for about two-thirds of the time. Carr and Amelia were "absent ... upwards of four months" and covered "almost three thousand miles" in 1796, while the trip to Wales also lasted "nearly four months." Uncle John Carr appears to have been indefatigable!

Finally, to round off the story, in his *Genealogy of the Family of the "Clarks"*, dated 1890, their nephew. C.F.G. Clark, whose initials appear after a marginal note in Amelia's diary, wrote: " ... four daughters were the beauties of the County, and as their great uncle (Alderman Carr, of York) had no children, he took them under his guidance and patronage, and introduced them to the best society in the county. They all married rich husbands, had numerous families, and died at a good old age."

Harriet was married to Thomas Swann, a banker of York, on 13th July 1796 and had one son and three daughters. She died on 1st July 1812, aged 36. Amelia married William Rayner, cloth merchant of Horbury, on St. Valentine's Day, 1804. She bore two sons and one daughter and died, aged 63, on 14th November 1841.

References

1. Colvin, H.,
    A Biographical Dictionary of British Architects, 1660-1840
    Yale University Press, London and New York, 1995, 3rd edition.

2. Worsley, G.,
    Crediting Carr
    Country Life, pp. 162-165, May 5, 1988

3. Worsley, G.,
    John Carr's Last Tour - A Romantic Excursion of 1805
    Country Life, pp. 132-133, April 10, 1987

Harriet Clark's Journal of the Tour made in the year 1795

June 1st Set out from York and dined at Ferrybridge, arrived to Tea at Mr. Hoylands[1], where we staid all night, and next day we dined with
2nd Miss Hinchliffe at Carlton and drank Tea at new Lodge[2] and return'd to Carlton; the next day we dined at New Lodge, and on the
4th day following we drank Tea with Miss Montjoy, and I staid at Carlton until the 8th. My Uncle went to Hickleton[3] on the 4th and
8th I went with Miss Hinchcliffe to Wentworth house[4] on the 8th where we staid a fortnight to enjoy the Grounds & beautiful prospects which are adorn'd with fine lakes of water & the most magnificent Woods in the Kingdom. About a Mile from the house stands the Grand Monument[5] of one hundred feet in height lately erected to the memory of the late Marquis of Rockingham by Earl Fitzwilliam, within which is a beautiful Statue of the Marquis of Rockingham, and in the surrounding niches are placed the Bustos of the duke of Portland, Lord John Cavendish, Admiral Keppel, Mr. Montague, Mr. Burke, Mr. Fox, Mr. Lee & Sir George Savile. The outside architecture and the inside finishing of this building, which was design'd by my Uncle, are very much admired; the Pyramidal building[6] is also a noble land mark, and the great Column[7] in Scoles wood, which was also design'd by my uncle, is the largest Column in Europe, being 17 feet in diameter, and 136 feet in height. The monument above mentioned is so situated as to command a view of every beautiful object around this grand place.

The whole front of the House, which is 612 feet long, is distinctly seen from this building, and it is one of the finest pieces of architecture in this Kingdom, particularly the Center part thereof; the noble Portico consists of eight Columns and two pilasters of the Corinthian order from which you enter into a magnificent Hall 60 feet square and 43 feet high, on each side of which are three noble rooms, superbly finish'd and adorn'd with fine pictures and Statues, beyond the power of my description; there is also a beautiful Chapel adorn'd with the pictures of our Saviour and the twelve apostles,[8] and a noble Gallery 126 feet in length. Mrs. Cross, the housekeeper, told me when the family was there, they made up 160 Beds; this circumstance shows the extent of this magnificent palace within, but the External Grandeur and the magnitude of the beautiful park and noble woods which surround the house cannot be described by my pen.

The noble Quadrangle of Stables [designed by my Uncle Carr] which are built round a Court of two hundred feet square ought not to be

Wentworth Woodhouse

2

omitted from my description of this noble place, as they are the most extensive and Safe buildings in the Kingdom, adjoining to which is a magnificent Riding School one hundred and thirty five (feet) in length and forty five feet in width.[9]

During our Stay at Wentworth house we visited the Temple in Tankersley Park [designed also by my Uncle Carr][10], the views from which are the most beautiful and extensive in the Kingdom; the same day we drank tea at Rotherham, which is a black, dirty town, in the Center of which is a most beautiful Gothick Church built by Bishop Rotherham.[11] Near this Town we saw a fine body of Yeoman Cavalry reviewed, commanded by Earl Fitzwilliam. Another day we Visited Wentworth Castle,[12] the seat of the Earl of Strafford, which is most certainly a beautiful place, and finely adorn'd with woods & water, and the views from the Castle behind the house are very grand and extensive. The West front of the house is a beautiful design, and the Sash frames being gilt give it a very brilliant appearance. The disposition and dimensions of the rooms within the house are not equal to the external appearance of the building, but there is a Gallery of 140 feet in length by 22 feet in width, within which are some good paintings.

From this place we visited Mr. Thwaites at Courtfield[13] where we drank tea and some excellent Cowslip wine made by his nieces. The house commands a beautiful and extensive view over the finest cultivated country in the Kingdom. Wortley lodge[14] is near this place, which belongs to the Countess of Bute. Swinton pottery[15] engaged our attention another day which is well worth seeing, the process of which is very ingenious & entertaining. I shall long remember with pleasure this visit to Wentworth house, not only for the hospitable entertainment which I met with there, but for the pleasure I also enjoy'd in seeing one of the finest Countrys in the world and the various beautiful scenes which surround this magnificent palace.

June 22nd   We left Wentworth house and went to Hardwicke hall, a noble old fabrick belonging to the duke of devonshire, where we staid three days; the house was built by the Countess of Shrewsbury in the reign of Queen Elizabeth, and under the Care of the said Countess, Mary Queen of Scots was kept prisoner 17 years. Her bed room where she slept and a great deal of her needle work is to be seen at this place. The house stands in the Center of an extensive park, stocked with a vast number of beautiful deer; there is a noble terrace round the park, from which many beautiful views may (be) seen at a distance, and in the deep valley below the house. The Rooms are exceeding large and spacious within the house, many of which are hung with Tapestry, and the others finish'd with Wainscott and Stucco in a very antient and Grotesque manner, particularly the Gallery which is 180 feet long, and into the recess

40 feet wide, and betwixt which 24 feet wide; there is another room much admired which remains standing in the old house called the Giants' room, the length of which is 55 feet 4 inches, 30 feet 6 inches wide, and 24 feet 9 inches high; this is thought a very fine proportion'd room.

At this place I met with an account of the above mentioned Countess of Shrewsbury, who was daughter of John Hardwicke of Hardwicke Esq.; she was married at fourteen to Robt. Barlow Esq. of derbyshire who left her all his fortune. Her second husband was Sir Wm. Cavendish, by whom she had three sons and three daughters. Her third husband was Sir Wm. St. Lowe of Glocestershire who left her all his Estate. Her fourth husband was the Earl of Shrewsbury whom she survived 17 years. Her second son, William Cavendish, was first Earl of devonshire; her third Son, Charles Cavendish, was Father to the duke of Newcastle. The oldest daughter, Frances, married Sir Henry Pierrepont, from whom the dukes of Kingston are descended. Her second daughter, Elizabeth, (was) married to Charles Stewart, Brother to King James I's father, and Mary, the third daughter, married Gilbert Talbot, afterwards Earl of Shewsbury. She built Chatsworth, Hardwick, Old Coates, Welbeck and Bolsover.[16] She died on the 13th of Feb. 1607, & was upwards of 90 years old.

From Hardwick we passed through Chesterfield [which is a well built town] in our way to Chatsworth; the prodigious mountains and Craggy rocks which we passed over, and the deep Ravines full of water falls astonish'd me very much before we reach'd Chatsworth.[17] The house which surrounds a noble Court is a magnificent building, and the situation charm'd and astonish'd me beyond anything I had ever seen. The grand mountain which rises into the Clouds on the East side of the house is finely covered with woods, on the bosom of which stands a beautiful Rustick building from every part of which there flows such a stream of water as to float over a magnificent Cascade with astonishing rapidity; this grand scenery and the jete d'eau, which throws up the water 90 feet high, is kept running during the dinner time on public days which are every Monday when the Duke is at Chatsworth.

In the cellars at Chatsworth we saw the twelve magnificent strong beer Casks which were made and filled with strong beer against the arrival of King William III, and on his landing at Torbay their contents were distributed to the populace assembled for the purpose of drinking his health before the Front of the house at Chatsworth. The casks are call'd the 12 Apostles and have the King's arms beautifully carved on the end of each cask. The noble family of Cavendish were the principal instruments in bringing about the glorious revolution and setting the Prince of Orange on the English Throne.

On the West side of the house the Rapid River derwent runs winding through the most picturesque park I ever beheld, one end of which terminates with a scene of huge Rocks magnificently grand and horrible, the other end runs into a beautiful Valley called darley dale which extends to Matlock. The rising ground of the Park and the Surrounding mountains are so near the house that every object on them may be distinctly seen, which was a great comfort to me, and they are most beautifully covered with deer and Cattle, hanging woods & scattered Trees, Villages and Rocks which look like ruins.

The rooms in the middle of the house are very grand & spacious, particularly the third story from the Ground. All the Ceilings thereof are beautifully painted by Vario[18] and the festoons of carving in every room by Gibbons[19] are wonderfully fine. [There are a few very fine paintings.] On the second Story there is a very grand Painted hall, and a beautiful Gallery, and the dining room, drawing room and Music room have been lately fitted up and elegantly furnished with damask & Gilded work.

During my stay here, which was about three weeks, we made excursions to Haddon house,[20] an antient seat belonging to the duke of Rutland, & to Matlock. The approach up the valley to Haddon house along the course of the River Wye is beautifully picturesque; the house stands embosomed with woods, through which the battlements and broken towers peep through the trees and remind one of an enchanted Castle. There is a long Gallery within the house with a Curious picture over the Chimney but nothing else worth mentioning.

The situation of Matlock is beautifully grand, Romantick & singular, arising from the combin'd effect of hanging woods, magnificent Rocks, and a rapid River running through the bottom of this deep Glen or Ravine, which are distinctly seen from the publick houses and walks on the opposite side of the Vale, and from whence you may descend by winding paths to the banks of the River, where Charon attends to Row you over to the opposite shore into the hanging woods; here winding walks are made that lead you along this beautiful scenery to the sight of Mr. Arkwright's Elegant house,[21] which stands on a charming Knowl and commands a view of his Cotton mills and a pretty little Church which he has built in the Valley below; from this Romantick scenery (we) return'd to Chatsworth, the beauties of which we enjoy'd with inexpressible pleasure for a few days before we set out for Buxton, which I fear'd would prove a dreary place after having so long enjoyed the beautiful scenes above described.

The Road from Chatsworth to Buxton is wild and Romantick beyond description; Middleton dale in particular is the most sublime and astonishing work of nature I had ever beheld, the stupendous and

Farnley Hall

Bastion-like form of the Rocks which seem to hang over you are wonderful & Terrific, the tops of some of which are beautifully adorn'd with wild shrubs and trees, and at the foot of which runs a murmering stream through this astonishing scenery.

I found Buxton a much more Christian-like place than I expected from the description I had heard of it; the noble buildings in the form of a Crescent, and the Octangular Stables first attract our notice, as they are buildings of such magnitude and beauty as I had never before seen and the Grand Mountains and deep Ravines which surround the place are wonderfully astonishing & singular. [These noble buildings were designed by my Uncle Carr 1784.][22] During my stay here I visited a place call'd Poole's hole which is a dismal, dark Cavern of a vast extent and magnitude within the bowels of the Earth. We staid at Buxton a fortnight, during which time I had the pleasure of meeting with Mrs. Rose from London, a charming woman with whom I enjoy'd the amusements of the place with great pleasure.

July 25th   On the 25th of July we left this place at six oClock in the morning, Breakfasted at Middleton, dined and staid all night at Sheffield, set out at six oClock in the morning and travell'd over the most beautiful country I ever saw to new Lodge, near Barnsley, to Breakfast - New Lodge is a beautiful place which belongs to my Uncle Carr;[23] (we) dined for the first time in the new house and in the Evening visited Miss Hinchliffe at Carlton. The next morning I came with my Uncle to Wakefield and was at the Musical opening of the new Church and other amusements that week, after which I went with Mrs. Carr and my Uncle James to Carr lodge where I enjoy'd with great pleasure the sweets of that delightful Country, and on the following Sunday I play'd the Organ at my Uncle Carr's request at Horbury Church.[24]

August 17th   We left Carr lodge, and went to Otley, where I met my dear Parents and my Sister Amelia. About a mile from Otley on the top of Otley Shiven is one of the grandest Views in the County; that summit commands the noble valley of Wharfdale, and from which you see Lord Harewood's house, Mrs Arthington's, Mr. Fawkes', and Sir James Ibbetson's noble house. [These houses were all design'd by my Uncle Carr.][25] Otley is a neat small town and Mr. Wilson's house is charmingly situated and commands a fine view of the Bridge and River Wharfe.

August 18th   On Thursday morning the 18th of August we set out with my Sister Amelia added to our party and went to Bolton Abbey where we dined with the Reverend Mr. Carr[26] who show'd us all the beautys of that charming Vale, in which stand the noble remains of Bolton Abbey which belongs to his Grace the duke of devonshire. From this place we passed through Skipton and slept at Gargrave; this part of Craven is beautiful in verdure and the long-horned Cattle with which this country Abounds are beautiful beyond any Cattle I had ever seen. we hired a Guide at Gargrave to conduct us through the charming Valley call'd Malhamdale to Gordall scar. The astonishing scenery in the approach to this grand Phenomenon of nature call'd Gordall is beyond the power of any description; the Rocks which surround you are upwards of one hundred yards in height, and project beyond their Base almost as much as they are in height and from the very top of these amazing Rocks there pours down a mighty torrent of water with incredible impetuosity which fills the whole of the Chasm betwixt these magnificent Rocks; but the water in its fall, being interrupted by intermediate Rocks, produces a very grand appearance by struggling to get through them to the bottom of the Gulph, where it divides into two streams that run over the rocks through the Valley below, until they meet the Chrystal stream which issues from the bottom of the Magnificent Rock call'd Malham Cove which is about a mile from Malham Town. The united streams are the source of the River Air which runs through Leeds. Malham Cove is a grand piece of Rockwork but very inferior to Gordall. In the Evening we reach'd Settle, a small inanimate Town, overhanging which is a noble Rock, the foreground to which is now (being) ornamented with walks and Shrubs by the Gentlemen of the Town.

August 20th   On the 20th we went to Kirby Londsdale to dinner; this Town is situated on the banks of the River Lune, and from the Churchyard there is a most delightful view of this animated River winding through the Vale below. In the Evening we reach'd Kendall, where our friend Mr Rigge[27] met us from Hawkshead; here we furnish'd ourselves with Scotch plaids which we found very useful to us on our journey. The town is well built, many good shops in it, and a very slippery pavement.

August 21st   On the 21st we travell'd over many enormous mountains before we came in sight of the grand Lake call'd Windermeer; we ascended to the top of one of the highest mountains, from whence we saw the whole extent of this magnificent piece of Water, which is 15 miles in length and upwards of One mile in breadth; the surrounding mountains, hanging woods and scattered white houses which adorn the banks of this noble Lake form the grandest scene I had ever Beheld; we descended the hill to Bowness and from thence went along a beautiful shady road to Low wood where we dined on the margin of the Lake and afterwards went by the Bishop of Llandaff's[28] and through Ambleside to Keensground, near Hawkshead, to tea, where our friend Mr. Rigge received us with inexpressible Civility. The Road from Low wood to Hawkshead is beautiful beyond description and from Keensground, where we staid a week with our friends, we had a charming view of the beautiful Lake call'd Easthead water round which we Rode through the hanging woods which surround and adorn the banks of this Lake.

August 24th   On the 24th we paid a morning visit to Mr. and Mrs. Strickland who live at the foot of Coniston grand Lake[29] nine miles in extent, and half a mile in breadth; the grand mountains call'd Coniston Fells which surround this Lake are very sublime & magnificent.

August 26th   On the 26th we dined with Mr. and Mrs. Strickland in consequence of their polite request, in order to enjoy a second view of this noble Lake and its astonishing Environs.

August 27th   On the 27th we visit Sr. Michael Fleming's seat at Rydal,[30] which is a situation truly singular and picturesque; the house is surrounded with the most magnificent woods, within which are several beautiful Cascades and winding walks which lead to the several waterfalls, one of which is seen from a Grotto which has the most solemn and sublime appearance of any thing I had ever seen. In this Grotto we ate, with much pleasure, our morning's repast and left this charming place with much reluctance.

August 28th   The next day we paid a morning Visit to Mr. and Mrs. Curwen on the great Island in the middle of Windermeer Lake,[31] who politely show'd us the house and pleasure grounds, the whole of which containing forty Acres so beautifully laid out with shrubs & walks by Mr. White. The round house I don't admire, but all together it is a most charming place & very different from anything I had ever seen.

August 29th   The next day we accepted Mr. and Mrs. Curwen's polite invitation to dine with them, previous to which we sail'd round the Island and spent a very pleasant day. On our way to this noble Lake we ascended a very high Rocky mountain, from which we had a complete View of this magnificent Lake, and its surrounding woods & Rocky mountains which are too astonishing and sublime for me to pretend to describe.

August 30th   The day following we dined with Mr. Braithwaite, and our friends at Bellemount;[32] he is the Rector of Hawkshead, & his house commands a charming view of Easthead Lake.

August 31st   We left our friends at Keensground and proceeded towards Keswick in Cumberland. We visited the Lakes of Grassmeer, Thirlemeer and Leeswater, dined at Mr. Curwen's shooting house at Wythburn,[33] and afterwards went through the sweet Vale of St. John's and arrived at Keswick (with) time enough to go to the Station near the Parsonage house which commands the finest view of the Lake of derwentwater and the Sugar Loaf mountains which surround this beautiful transparent

Rydal Waterfall and Bridge

10

Lake. From the above mentioned Station we had also a fine view of Basingthwaite water which is beautifully skirted with a hanging wood on one side, and noble mountains on the other. But the spiral pointed mountains call'd Borrowdale Fells which surround the lake of Derwentwater exceed in singularity any scene I had ever before met with. We visited this Evening we were at Keswick, Mr. Crosthwaite's Museum of natural curiosity in which are many things well worth seeing, particularly a large fine toned Indian Conch. The house and other buildings Erected by Mr. Pocklington upon the Island in the Lake are too ugly to be taken notice of.[34]

September 1st   We left Keswick and travell'd by Saddleback and the Grand mountain call'd Skiddaw to Ulswater. This noble Lake is only inferior to Windermeer. It is about nine miles long and about a mile in breadth; from the top of Dunmail there is a noble view of the whole lake and its environs.

At Patterdale at the end of Ulswater not long ago lived one Parson Mallison, who having a few acres of land of his own was call'd the King of Patterdale and he was Minister of the place 60 years & died lately at the age of ninety. [My Uncle Carr knew this clergyman.] During the early part of his life his benefice brought him in only £12 a year; by degrees it became worth £18 a year which it never exceeded. On this income he married, brought up four children, lived comfortably among his neighbours, educated a Son at College and left upwards of a thousand pounds behind him. He himself read the burial service over his mother; he married his father to a second wife and afterwards he buried him also. He publish'd his own Banns of Marriage in the Church with a woman whom he had christened, and himself married all his children. From this specimen the manners of the County may easily be conceived; at a distance from the refinements of the age, they are at a distance from its views, and though ignorance is sometimes call'd the mother of vice, I apprehend it to be as often the nurse of Innocence.

We dined at the foot of the Lake at Poolley Bridge, and in the Evening we travell'd by delmain house,[35] through the sweet Vale of Eamont to Penrith which is a well built Town. There is a handsome Church, the Gallerys in which are supported by Red stone Columns.

September 2nd   On the 2nd of September We set out for Carlisle, dined at Heskett Castle and arrived at Carlisle (with) time enough to see the Castle and all its fortifications, Cannon & Batterys which appear'd very singular to me; this antient City is beautifully situated at the conflux of the Solway Firth, the River Petterell and the River Eden. The Cathedral Church is a noble Gothick building in the style & form of York Minster, within which is a small Church commonly made use of.

September 3rd   We set out for Scotland, breakfasted at Longtown and went from thence to Springfield, a small village adjoining Gretna Green where the Blacksmith lives who performs the marriage ceremony. We saw his house and Wife but the Bishop - as he is call'd - was invisible to us.

September 4th   On the 4th we travell'd over very inanimate dreary Country to Agglefechon where we dined and staid all night; the next morning we set out towards Cudwoody green in the County of Dunfrize where we breakfasted, & proceeded through Lochaby, a market town, to Moffat, which is a neat Market town and much frequented as a watering place on account of the Sulphur springs near the Town. The Country for many miles before we came to Moffat is finely cultivated, very good roads and a great many very large woods and young plantations.

From Moffat our next Stage was to Elvinfoot; we set out at Seven in the morning and travell'd over the highest and most tremendous mountains I ever beheld, during which it poured down with rain, but we shut ourselves up in the Phaeton until the rain abated, and I mounted my horse again. Immediately afterwards I was passed by two gentlemen in a Chaise who politely desired I would take a Corner of it to Elvinfoot as it was likely to rain again; at the request of my Uncle I got into the Chaise and was very much pleased with the description of the Country which they gave me, until we arrived at Elvinfoot, the very worst Inn I ever was at; we breakfasted of mouldy bread, Eggs, sweetmeats and Tea for which we paid as much as we should in St. James street. However, we dined with Duke Humphrey,[36] and in the Evening arrived at a good house, [near Lord Douglas's seat][37] called Douglas Mill, an Odd house where we got a gay supper and retired early to rest.

The next day we travell'd a great many miles along the banks of the River Clyde towards Lanark, the County town of Lanarkshire, about two miles short of which town we turned out of the Road to see the magnificent falls of the River Clyde which run through the Woods and alongside of Lady Ross's park, the widow of the late Sir John Lockart Ross, the Admiral.[38] It is impossible to describe by any words the astonishing Effect which these grand Cataracts and the surrounding scenery of Rocks and woods have upon the mind; at first sight I was struck with surprise and horror at the terrific appearance of a noble River coming tumbling down from one huge Rock to another with incredible foam and fury for half a mile in extent. The banks are adorn'd with hanging woods and walks rudely cut out, and seats properly placed where you may rest and enjoy this wonderful Scenery. The Grotto and an old Mill surrounded with foaming water had a very picturesque Effect in the Center of this astonishing scene.

We dined at Lanark at an excellent Inn, built at the expense of the Country; there is a handsome Church, but few good houses. After dinner we set out for Hamilton, and about two miles from Lanark we were astonished and attracted to the Riverside by the tremendous roaring of the River Clyde from an astonishing Cataract below which stands a very large Cotton Mill. The Road from Lanark to Hamilton, about 16 miles along the banks of the Clyde, is beautiful beyond description, & adorn'd with noble woods and Gentlemen's seats, Captain Nesbitt's & Captain Hamilton's[39] are charming Situations, & Lord Hindford's Gothick house[40] is a handsome building. I cannot avoid mentioning again the last grand Cataract we saw in our road to Hamilton. It is certainly more singular and Terrific than that near Lady Ross's house, though not so extensive.

It was late in the Evening when we arrived at Clark's Inn at Hamilton. In the morning we went to see the Duke of Hamilton's house and Park[41] which are very near the Town. It is a large comfortable house, and in the Gallery are some good paintings, particularly that of 'David in the Lion's Den'.

From Hamilton we proceeded through a beautiful country some 11 miles to Glasgow; we passed by a pretty place belonging to Lord douglas[42] in our way to Glasgow, the Suburbs of which extend 4 miles before we reach'd this noble City, which is in the County of Lanark.

The town is exceeding well built and the streets wide and regular and extremely populous; the whole place seems in a Bustle with Carriages and horses. We went to see the College which is an Antient black building & the students' apartments very small; the great Library and Hall are handsome, & there are a few good paintings. The general Infirmary and the Tradesmen's hall are very handsome modern buildings & the Saxon Church of St. Mungo is a very singular building of great antiquity, within which are two places of worship, one above the other, and the upper Church is divided into two distinct parts, which belong to distinct parishes of dissenters, which is the religion of the Country.

The town Class of women go half naked, without Shoes or Stockings hats or Cloaks, in short, half a bedgown & small pettycoat, and sometimes a little plaid, is all their dress, and they carry heavy burthens, and do all the drudgery while the Men are well clad and lounging in the streets & are too Idle even in Harvest time to go to work in the fields.

In our rambles we saw the four handsome Bridges which Cross the Clyde, which runs on one side of the City, near which is a publick place call'd the green park laid out in walks & planted with trees to a vast extent, in the Center of which is a spacious publick wash house of great magnitude in which all the linen in the town is wash'd and Ironed. We visited the Assembly Room at a noble Inn call'd the Tontine but were much disappointed as it is a very small, inelegant Room. The Merchants' Hall is a noble modern room 75 feet long, 35 feet wide and 90 feet high,

Hamilton Palace

14

adjoining to which are several handsome rooms where the different trades meet. The muslin & other manufactorys carried on at this place are very considerable, some of which we saw.

The first morning after we left Glasgow we slept at Cumbernaud, a single house near Lord Elphinston's seat,[43] a neat flat place; he is the owner of an immense tract of land in this country which is flat and inanimate; we past through Kylsyth and Kirkintulach and over some dangerous drawbridges over the great Canal from the Clyde to the Forth, and arrived the next day at Sterling, in our road to which place we passed by many Gentlemen's houses prettily situated; Mr. Marsden's, Mr. Monro's, Mr. Ship's & others.[44]

St Ninnion's is a Curious Town two miles short of Sterling; all the outsides of the houses & shops are painted with the commodities which they sell within; the country round this Town is beautiful and finely cultivated.

On our arrival at Sterling we went to see the Castle which had long attracted our attention by its magnificent situation upon an amazing high Rock, inaccessible on every side but that towards the City. In our way to this stupendous building we were observ'd by an old but very polite officer to be strangers, and he very courteously staid with us and show'd us all the fortifications and apartments in which the King of Scotland sometimes lived; he showed us also the surprising windings of the river Forth which to a little village call'd Aloa is 24 miles by water, and only four by road. The Views on every side from the top of the Castle are surprisingly Grand & extensive, Benlomond and many other noble hills have a grand appearance. We had the assembly room for our dining room at sterling, and our apartments over it and our entertainments, particularly the Scots soop was very good.

The country from this place to the Iron works at Carron is very beautiful. We saw the whole apparatus of these astonishing Iron works,[45] the infernal regions I had read of seem'd realiz'd by the roaring of the bellows and the dreadful fires, out of which the liquid metal issued & was cast into various forms by such figures of Men as I had never before seen.

From this place we passed through Falkirk, Motherbourn, and the seat of the late General dundas, who was just dead of the yellow fever in the West Indies. Kerse is near Falkirk, the seat of the late Sr. Lawry Dundas.[46]

In the afternoon we arrived at Linlithgow, a very antient City, in which stands the remains of a noble palace, the principal residence of James I, and James IV; the whole building was habitable in the year 1745, but the King's Army set fire to it during the rebellion, and ran away for fear of the Rebels who had advanced to Falkirk. We were in the small house in which Mary Queen of Scots was born. Behind the Palace is a noble Lake of water which we saw from the top of the palace and from which place we had a fine view of the noble River Forth running onwards to Edinburgh [This lake is call'd Linlithgow Loch]. In the Centre of the Market place there stands one of the most beautiful Fountains in the world, from which eighteen chrystal streams of pure water perpetually run. Near this Fountain stands a noble old Sessions house.

In this neighbourhood are many Gentlemen's seats, viz. Callender, belonging to Mr. Forbes,[47] Major General Maxwell's at Park hill, and many others in beautiful situations & which have a fine View of an Arm of the Sea. We spent many pleasant days at this place, where we had the assembly rooms for our dining Room and our apartments at one end thereof.

The next morning we set out towards Edinburgh; we Breakfasted at Kirkliston, (where) from the Churchyard is a very pretty view of the River Annon. From the Tombstones in this Churchyard we observed that a woman after marriage does not change her Maiden name to that of her husband. Part of the Church is Saxon Architecture. Near this place stands Hoptown house, a very antient Fabrick,[48] and also several small Seats belonging to the Dundas familys.[49]

September 12th   The whole road was beautiful to Edinburgh where we arrived at two oClock on the 12th September at Mr. Walker's Hotel in the new Town near the Bridge where we had charming apartments and excellent provisions sent us from his Brothers who keep the opposite Hotel.

Edinburgh is situated upon a steep rising hill from East to West and terminates with an inaccessible Rock upon which the Castle stands; at the East end or lower part of the City, distant from the Castle about a mile, stands the Abbey of Holyrood House or the King's Palace. Betwixt them, almost in a line, runs the high street, on the South side of which rise Salisbury rocks and Arthur's seat, a hill of about 800 feet of perpendicular height, and to the North, Calton hill is situated but is considerably lower than Arthur's Seat, so that the situation of this City is most singular and Romantic, lying betwixt two hills, and the Castle may be call'd a third hill as it overlooks the Town and is little inferior in height to the highest of the other two. The houses in the high street have a dirty appearance and few of them are less than Eleven storys high, some of them are ten storys high towards the street, and fourteen in the back part thereof.

The new Town was projected in 1752[50] and is now almost finished, and from the advantages of the situation, and being regularly built hath undoubtedly a beautiful Effect, but its situation is remarkably exposed to storms of wind which, I am told, sometimes rage from the Firth of Forth with uncommon violence. The New Town, as it is call'd, consists of three straight streets almost a mile in length which are intersected at right angles with several cross streets. One of these streets is call'd Queen street and is 100 feet in width; this being nearest the River, has a charming view of the River and the shipping moving upon it, and of the fine County of Fifeshire. [The Centre house with Colms. to it was designed by my Uncle Carr].[51] George street, which is in the middle, is no less than 115 feet wide and is terminated at one end with St. Andrews square & at the other end with Charlotte square. Prince's street is the most Southerly, only one side of which is built.

The new Bridge, which united the communication betwixt the old and new Town was built in the year 1770, is 40 feet wide in the middle and 50 feet at each end. The Register Office fronts the end of the new bridge and is 200 feet in length and 80 feet deep, in the center of which is a Saloon 50 feet diameter and 80 high, lighted by a top light only 15 feet in diameter. There is a projecting stone Gallery, round within, with recesses in the wall for the Records. Upon a pedestal on the floor is a Statue of the present King executed in white marble by the Hon. Mrs. Damer. It is a clumsy looking Statue. We were told this building cost forty thousand pounds. It was by Mr. Adams, plann'd & executed.[52]

The Exchange is a handsome building round a Court with Piazzas one side where people can walk under cover, the other sides are shops. The Amphitheatre is 60 feet (in) diameter and will hold 1500 spectators; the Equestrian exploits, dancing and tumbling are the same as Astleys in London.

Holyrood house is the only Royal palace in Scotland that is not in ruins. The building surrounds a Court of 230 feet square with piazzas on each side thereof, the Gateway into which is handsome with double Columns supporting a Cupola. The great Gallery within is 150 feet long and 27 wide and is hung around with the supposed Portraits of all the Kings of Scotland. The unfortunate Queen Mary's bed of Crimson damask, bordered with green fringe and tassels, is still to be seen, and her dressing room & private closet. Lord darnley, her husband, and his assassins entered into the private closset, dragg'd out Rizzio through her bed Chamber, and murdered him in her dressing room; the blood upon the floor where he was stabb'd by their daggers is very visible to this day. This unhappy Victim was secretary to the Queen and an Eminent Italian musician, and was at supper with the Queen & the dutchess of Argyl. A great deal of this building was burnt by Cromwell's Soldiers, but was repair'd to its present form after the restoration.

The Castle stands on a high Rock accessible only towards the Town; you enter it by a draw bridge and Gate which is defended by two batteries of Cannon; beyond this there are two more Gateways, very

Royal Bank of Scotland

18

strong and with two portcullises of Iron with spikes which can be dropp'd down. The whole is defended with a great many brass cannons carrying Balls from 12 to 18 pounds weight. There is a large square built round with houses for the Officers' lodgings and also Baracks which will contain a thousand Soldiers and an Arsenal to contain 8000 stand of Arms.

There are also Royal apartments, in one of which we saw the room where James VI was born. The Regalia formerly kept here which belong'd to the King is supposed to be now in the Tower at London as the room where it was kept, I was told, has not been opened since the Union. The Governour's Salary is a thousand pounds a year and the Deputy Governour's five hundred. The Castle is at present defended by a company of Invalids and about 500 regulars.

The view from the platform where the Flag staff stands is the most noble and extensive I ever beheld, you see distinctly Sterling castle and have a charming view of the Sea and all the shipping in Leith harbour, and the innumerable scattered houses along the banks of the Forth and in Fifeshire, which are chiefly Gentlemen's seats appear beautiful beyond description.

The parliament house is a magnificent old building. The hall is 123 feet long and 42 broad with an arched Roof of Oak, below which is one of the most valuable Libraries in great Britain belonging to the faculty of Advocates. Besides thirty thousand printed volumes, which were politely shown us by Mr. Gibbs, the Librarian, (there is) an intire Mummy in its original chest given by the Earl of Morton which cost him £300. In the Court before the door is an Equestrian Statue of Charles II.[53]

We visited the old university, and St. James square, which is a handsome large Quadrangle, leading towards which are several handsome streets built in the old Town, and we saw the front now building for the new University which will be very handsome, design'd by Mr. Adam.[54]

Heriot's hospital is the most singular old fashion'd building I ever saw, and owes its foundation to one George Heriot, Goldsmith to James VI. He left £23,600 for the maintenance and bringing up of poor freemen's Sons of the town of Edinburgh in the year 1628. It stands in a beautiful situation and is distinctly seen from the Castle.

The Observatory is built on the top of Calton hill which is a delightful situation; around this hill there is a pleasant walk which affords the finest prospects that can be imagined, varying remarkably almost at every step. On this hill is a burying ground which contains a fine monument to the memory of david Hume, the historian [Hume was buried erect by his own desire. CRC] and on this beautiful hill a new Bridewell is also

Register Office, Scotland

erected in a kind of Gothick form, singular enough but having no claim to beauty or architecture.

We visited Leith and was astonished at the sight of so many large Ships riding at anchor in a safe harbour; this is defended from the sea by a long wall or mole upon which there is a charming walk and a delightful View of the Sea. From Edinburgh to Leith is about two miles. It is a charming walk, and adorn'd with pretty houses and Gardens almost all the way & has a fine view of the Sea.

September 17th   We left Edinburgh and came to Musselburgh where we saw an encampment of fencibles[55] on Fisher row Sand. It is a long, rambling, dirty Seaport town. We also passed by Prestonpans, a large Seaport town, and arrived in the Evening at a dirty inn at Haddington, a large old town; here is a noble Gothick Cathedral in Ruins prettily situated by the side of the River.

September 18th   At seven in the morning we set out after breakfast and arrived at Dunbar where we got, as usual, a second breakfast which is brought you with the Tea at every place in Scotland, to which we generally added Egg or Ham or Sweetmeats. This place is much resorted to for bathing in the Sea, and is a pretty well-built Market town, and here is a charming Inn built by Lord Lauderdale. [Lord Lauderdale's seat is near Dunbar.][56] We passed by a seat of Lord Harrington[57] and another large encampment of fencibles, and many pretty places in our way to Press Inn where we spent a pleasant Evening though it is an odd house, but a good Inn. The Road is beautiful all the way from Dunbar, the Country very hilly and full of deep Ravines, over one of which is a noble high Arch Bridge with an Iron Ballustrade to each side thereof. I remember we were almost two hours gathering shells among the Rocks near Dunbar & were very near being surrounded with the Tide.

This Country is finely cultivated and was full of fine corn ready to be cut, but very few Inhabitants to be seen. We were told that the Highlanders who usually come into these parts in Harvest time were all enlisted for Soldiers. Indeed, every town we went through was full of them. We passed by the Duke of Roxborough's seat[58] which appear'd a beautiful place, & the next day we reach'd Berwick upon Tweed, which is a dirty looking town, but the Ramparts and the fortifications are very grand & noble, with large batterys of Cannon upon them. Three sides of the City is surrounded by the Sea, and the River Tweed runs along the other side, over which, towards the South, is a Bridge of Fifteen arches. We walked round the Ramparts, from which the views of the Sea and the adjoining Country are beautiful, but I shall never forget the steep and dangerous ascent for four miles which we were obliged to travel on a paved Road immediately out of Berwick towards Belford, where we spent the Evening very pleasantly. Early in the morning we set out for Alnwick, which is a large market town with a pretty square market place.

Near this Town stands Alnwick Castle, one of the principal seats of the family of Percy, now Duke of Northumberland. It is situated on the South side of the River Alne over which is a beautiful stone bridge in sight of the Castle. The entrance from the town is through a dank, gloomy Gateway into the first Court of the Castle; from here you have a view of the whole building which is adorn'd with pinnacles, Towers, Battlements and a vast variety of figures upon them. You pass through a second & third court before you arrive at the Grand Citadel into which you enter by a grand staircase in the shape of a fan, 46 feet long, 35 feet wide and 43 feet high. The first room we entered was call'd the Saloon, 42 feet long, 37 feet wide, and 20 feet high, the finishing thereof in Stuco is in the most elegant Style of Gothick Architecture; the adjoining room to this is the drawing room in an Oval form, with a semicircular Bow on one side therefore. The room is 46 feet long, 35 feet wide and 22 feet high. The next room is the dining room, 54 feet long, 21 feet wide and 26 feet 9 inches high. To this room is a circular bow 19 feet diameter. This room is beautifully finished with Gothick Ornaments in Stuco. The library is a noble room, 64 feet, beautifully fitted up for books in a Gothick manner. But the Chapel exceeds all the other rooms in Gothick elegance; the great East window is beautiful beyond the power of my description; it is like the East window in York Minster, the Ceiling like that of King's College Chapel in Cambridge and the walls, I was told, are painted after the great Church at Milan. The whole Ornaments & Ceiling are beautifully Gilt, and the windows are beautifully illuminated with the finest painted Glass. The length of the Chapel is 50 feet by 21 foot 6 inches wide to which is a beautiful recess where the family sit. There are several very handsome Bed chambers and Circular dressing rooms.

The Castle with its Courts is flanked with sixteen towers and occupies a space, we were told, of five Acres and is said to be first founded in the times of the Romans, and was said to be an impregnable fortress before the invention of Cannon. Malcolme, the third King of Scotland, and his Son lost their Lives in attempting to take it in the reign of William Rufus, King of England. The park is very beautiful and the ground round the whole is charmingly laid out with walks & Shrubberys to a vast extent and there are noble planations made by the late duke.

We spent a very pleasant afternoon in viewing the Castle and its delightful Environs, and in the morning early we set out for Morpeth where we dined and spent the afternoon at a good Inn. It is a pretty little Town and there is a handsome Town house and a good Market place.

The Country round the Town is rather pretty. In our Road from Morpeth to Newcastle we passed by Sir Matthew White Ridley's, and Mr. Brandlings,[59]. The Country was pretty about Bligh.

I was disappointed with the appearance of Newcastle which is a very large, irregular built Town. The Gothick Tower of St. Nicholas Church attracts one's notice from the singularity of the upper part thereof being supported upon four arches rising from the four angles of the tower. This they are now cleaning & painting. We walked upon the Quay or Staith to see the shipping and the new Bridge which is much too narrow. The Assembly rooms are handsome and spacious. We were shown the walk around the town which is inanimate & unpleasant.

September 21st   On the 21st of September we reached Durham, which is a very dirty, irregular built Town, but charmingly situated, and the walks round which upon the banks of the River Weir are beautifully picturesque, and extremely like Matlock; from some points where you see the Elegant bridges I thought the scenery superior to many parts of Matlock. At the end of this charming walk, which is a mile in length, stands an antient church in ruins upon a hill, from which you have view of the Town, the noble Cathedral and the Bishop's Palace which is a very antique building with a new Gothick Gateway to it, design'd by My Uncle.[60] We went to the afternoon prayers, and heard Mr. Mason's little Anthem prettily sung by one of the Boys, and a fine Toned Organ very well play'd. The building seems very antient, partly Saxon and Gothick Architecture. The Saxon pillars are round and very clumsy. The Quire is handsome, but the whole is very inferior to York minster. We walked through the Cloysters which are singular and very convenient to walk in; the Prebendal houses, where the rich Prebends live, form a handsome square at the end of the Cloysters.

From Durham we passed through the long village of Chester le Street, from which place we had a fine view of Lumley Castle belonging to the Earl of Scarborough,[61] which seems finely situated; we also saw at a distance Hardwick, near Sedgfield, which now belongs to Mr. Russell,[62] and Sir John Eden at Windlestone[63] is about a mile from the Road upon a rising hill, but the Country is in general very flatt & inanimate and scarce a tree to be seen except about Hardwick and Windlestone. We spent the Evening at Darlington which is a pretty small well paved market town; there is a handsome Church and market place.

From Darlington we passed over Croft Bridge which is a very handsome structure on the River Tees, which divides the Counties of Durham and Yorkshire. We passed also through a pretty village call'd Scorton where there is a handsome School house & a pretty green before it, and arrived at Caterick Bridge where we breakfasted and afterwards

Sedbury Park, nr Gilling

went to Richmond, which is a most charming Situation alongside of which runs the Rapid river Swale. On the North side of the River the remains of an antient Castle stand, built by Alane, Earl of Bretagne, nephew of William the Conqueror, by whom Alane was created Earl of Richmond. There are the remains also of an antient Monastery, the tower part of which is very handsome and entire. The remains also of St. Martin's Monastery are to be seen, and about a mile from Richmond are the beautiful remains of Easby Abbey from which you have a beautiful view of the Town of Richmond & the River Swale.

After dinner I call'd on Miss Hogg, and we walked round the delightful Gardens belonging to Mr. York,[64] from which you have a charming view of the River and the handsome new Bridge designed by my Uncle. The Town is well built and paved and there is a handsome market place in which stands an ugly Obelisk.

From Richmond we went to Aske hall, the seat of Sir Thomas Dundas [now Lord Dundas],[65] the pleasure grounds round which and the Gothick Temple are very pretty, the view from the house confined. One may just see Sedbury, the seat of Sir Robert Darcy Hildyard[66] which stands on an Elevated situation near the Town of Gilling, where we paid a visit and drank tea with Mrs. Thistlethwaite, and return'd in the Evening to Caterick Bridge, an excellent Inn belonging to Sir John Lawson, whose seat at Brough is near this place.[67]

September 24th   In the morning of the 24th of September we passed by Hornby Castle which is a noble building and commands a very extensive prospect over the Vale of Mowbray as far as York.[68] [This Castle now belongs to the Duke of Leeds, on consequence of his marrying the Earl of Holderness's daughter].

We dined at Masham, a pretty small market town, around which the Country is very beautiful being full of woods, and the noble River Yure meandering through the Valley adds great beauty to the situation of Masham. We passed by Mr. Danby's of Swinton[69] on our way to Hackfall.

This place call'd Hackfall[70] is astonishingly singular and Grand from the united Effect of hanging woods, Romantic Rocks and a Rapid River rolling through the Center of the scenery. The hanging woods from their Convex and Concave appearance are amazingly singular, and they are very much intersected by deep Ravines through which rapid streams of water roll down and form a variety of Cascades, to which you are unexpectedly led by the Rude walks and through the woods to all the beautiful points of view of this Romantic scenery. Upon the summit of the hill above the woods are several seats and Grotesque buildings from which the best views may be seen of this charming place, but I was not satisfied with looking only one way down the valley, but I descended to the verge of the River into the bottom of the vale, from which every object seemed magnified and the scenery more astonishing.

We slept this Evening at Mrs. Haddon's at Ripon and early in the morning we set out for Studley Park,[71] where we breakfasted and afterwards saw all the beautiful scenes of this charming place which is much adorn'd with noble woods & elegant buildings and the walks and Shrubberys are beautiful, but the Grandest Scene in the place is the noble view of Fountains Abbey from the Gothick seat. The beautiful remains of this venerable structure were lately purchased of the Messenger family by the late Mr. Aislaby. The walls of the Church are very intire and also the Refectory and dormitorys, and the Cloysters have been very extensive; the building is said to be as antient as York Minster, the situation of which by the side of the River Skell is gloomy and solemn. On one side it is surrounded with a range of huge massive rocks, and the other is overhung with a venerable old wood & shrubs of various sorts.

In the close of the last Century a piece of human antiquity existed in the neighbourhood of this Abbey more Curious than the abbey itself, that venerable instance of longevity Henry Jenkins. Among the events which, in the course of one hundred and sixtynine years, had fastened on the memory of this singular Man he spoke of nothing with such emotion as the antient state of Fountains Abbey. If he was questioned on that subject he would be sure to inform you "what a place it had once been" and would speak with much feeling of the clamour which its dissolution occasioned in the country about 130 years ago. He would say "when I was Butler to Lord Conyers, and old Marmaduke Bradley Esq., now dead and gone, was the Lord Abbot, I was often sent by my Lord to enquire after the Lord Abbot's health, and the Lord Abbot would always send for me up to his Chamber, and would order me perhaps a quarter of a yard of Roast beef and a Wassel bowl, which I remember well was always brought in a black Jack." From this account we see what it was that Rivetted Fountains Abbey distinctly in the old Man's memory; the Roast beef and black Jack, I doubt not was a stronger Idea than all the splendour of the house or all the Virtues of the Lord Abbot.

From the Abbey we were conducted to a beautiful building called the Banqueting House, and from then into a Valley through which the River Skell meanders, which is very beautifully adorn'd with hanging woods, but the road through this Vale is almost impassable with a Carriage, and I was obliged to cross the River three times with great difficulty before we could get out of this singular Glen, the ascent out of which is very steep and dangerous, and particularly so to the Chinese Temple, the road to which is very narrow with a high bank on one side thereof and a precipice on the other of 300 feet in height. The danger I had encountered in driving the carriage up this precipice was dreadful to think of and I was very happy when I had got into the Park. From this place we were shown to the Glass House in the park, which commands a very extensive and beautiful view on every side therefore. Ripon Minster is a noble object in the foreground of this scene and York Minster terminates the view of the rich vale of Mowbray.

We return'd from this delightful place to Ripon to dinner, and arrived at Ellenthorp[72] to Tea, where I found all my dear relations in perfect health. After resting a few days I went to York with my Sister in the Phaeton to fetch a fresh assortment of clothes. We afterwards spent a very pleasant week at Ellenthorp with my parents and in visiting our friends at Boroughbridge Races, and on the 10th October we set out again for Buxton where we spent three weeks very agreeably. Miss Hinchliffe was of our party, and we lodged in the same house with Sr. John and Lady Lawson & Miss Wickam who were very good neighbours and extremely civil to me. Mr. and Mrs. Cookson and Miss Cookson from London were also very polite and attentive to us, and I had a great deal of pleasure in meeting the two Miss Listers at Buxton.

We returned from there to Wentworth house where we spent a week very agreably. Mr. Woodhead who we had often seen at Buxton was of the party who was an old acquaintance of Mr. Hall's.[73] On our return from Wentworth House we met my Father at New Lodge where we spent a Couple of days and from thence we return'd to Wakefield.

The week following we went to pay a visit to Mr. Lister and his Sisters at Shibdin Hall[74] near Halifax.

25th November   We went to see Manchester along with Miss Ann Lister; this is a charming well built large town and the approach to it from Rochdale is very handsome, particularly the footpath for those who walk; (it) is carefully protected and kept in repair the whole of the way from Rochdale to Manchester. We saw several of the Manufactorys, particularly the printing of the Cottons, and the drawing of their Velvets and other fine goods over an exceeding hot Iron Roller is very curious & surprising. I had the pleasure of calling on Mrs. Lever and Miss Winter who very politely attended us to several places. My Uncle bought Mrs. Carr of Wakefield a stuff Gown & Miss Hinchliffe a Muff and Tippet.[75]

During the Evening we were at Manchester, at the Bridgewater's Arms, a very deep snow fell which made our journey not so pleasant on our return to Shibden hall, but it is a charming road from Rochdale to Manchester by Middleton. Sr. Ashton Lever's house at Ackrington[76] stands prettily, and the new house built by Lord Grey de Wilton is a handsome building.[77] Rochdale is a black-looking town and stands upon very uneven ground and the country round it is unpleasant. The Road over Blackstone Edge is bleak and romantick, and from thence to Halifax by Ripponden & Sowerby is very singular and full of handsome buildings & inhabitants. It was dark on our return, but the whole road was illuminated with Cotton mills and other manufactorys for several miles before we reach'd Shibden hall.

The next day we went to Halifax and saw the magnificent Piece Hall which was design'd by my Uncle,[78] the new Church and several handsome buildings, and return'd to Mr. Lister's to dinner. The day following we went to dewsbury and dined with Mr. and Mrs. Marriott and return'd in the Evening to Wakefield. I cannot omit mentioning that the whole country is beautiful from Halifax to Wakefield. It is full of inhabitants, scattered Villages, noble hanging woods, and beautiful prospects, particularly towards Elland and Hudderfield. Shibden Hall where I spent some pleasant days, is the most Antique building I ever saw, and there is a Yew tree that is a great curiosity with an Archway cut through it and the top of it is cut into regular Embrassures. The valley is beautiful in which the house is situated, and the inhabitants of this Antique place are very worthy people.

We staid at Wakefield with Mr. and Mrs. Carr almost a fortnight where I spent my time very pleasantly with them, and was at the Concert one Evening with Miss Clough.

16th December   On the 16th of december we set out for York, dined at Ferrybridge, and arrived at home to Tea in perfect health, after an absence of one hundred and ninety nine days.

Footnotes - 1795

1. Probably Brierley Manor, a pre-Reformation house.
2. Near Barnsley; built by John Carr, c. 1795 and occupied by his nephew, John Clark.
3. Hickleton Hall, near Mexborough; c. 1780 John Carr made certain alterations to an earlier mansion for Wentworth Wentworth of Woolley, including Adam-style decorations.
4. Wentworth Woodhouse. Two disconnected eighteenth century houses merging into one another, one facing E., the other W.
5. The Rockingham Mausoleum, built between 1785 and 1791.
6. The Needle's Eye - 45 feet high, of ashlar blocks, with an ogee entrance arch and an ogee vault, surmounted by an urn.
7. Keppel's Column, begun in 1773, finished by 1778 and payment completed in 1781. Begun as a folly, completed as a monument in memory of the acquittal at court martial of Admiral Keppell.
8. Said by Pevsner to be "in Rubens's style."
9. Built betweem 1766 and c. 1782 in the back range of the stables.
10. Presumably "Lady's Folly", now derelict and falling down. Pevsner describes it as a 2-storeyed building with, on the upper floor to north and south, three arches separated by attached Tuscan columns; lower extension to east and west. Pyramid roof.

11. All Saints'. The south chancel chapel was built by Thomas Rotherham of Lincoln in 1480.

12. The E. range was built after Thomas Wentworth (first Earl of Stafford of the second creation) bought the estate in 1708; the south and west ranges date from c. 1760-65.

13. So far it has been impossible to trace Courtfield, or to find where Miss Hinchcliffe lived in Carlton. There was a farmhouse known as Carlton Hall, near Rothwell, Wakefield, which is not far from Carlton, which had associations with the Savile family.

14. John, 3rd Earl of Bute, (Prime Minister and First Lord of the Treasury, 1762-68) on 27th August 1736, married Mary, only daughter of Edward Wortley-Montagu of Wortley, Co. Yorks. On 3rd April 1761 she was created Baroness Mount Stuart of Wortley. She died in 1794.

15. The Rockingham Pottery was established in 1745, closing in 1842.

16. In 1553 Bolsover was granted by the Crown to Sir George Talbot, 6th Earl of Shrewsbury, husband to 'Bess of Hardwick', whose son Charles, by her second marriage to William Cavendish, purchased the castle and manor from the 7th Earl.

17. The present house was built by William Talman for the 1st Duke of Devonshire between 1687 and 1707.

18. Antonio Verrio (1630-1707), the Neapolitan artist whose self-portrait may be seen at Beningbrough. He made his name in France before coming to England in 1671; he was appointed 'Chief and First Painter to the King' in 1684, having worked at Whitehall Palace, Windsor Castle and Hampton Court.

19. Grinling Gibbons (1648-1721); born in Rotterdam of English parents; about 19 when he came to York to work with William Etty, the carver. Charles II appointed him 'Master Carver in Wood to the Crown', a post he held until 1714.

20. Haddon Hall, now dating back some 600 years.

21. Cromford Old Mill. Richard Arkwright (1732-1792), patented a water-powered spinning machine in 1767.

22. Built between 1779-1784 for the 6th Duke of Devonshire in order to promote the town as a spa. The stables date from 1784-1785.

23. Carr Lodge, Horbury, was originally called *Sun Royd*. Built c. 1765 by Joseph Bayldon and bought by John Carr in 1789 for his nephew, John Carr, who was an attorney.

24. St. Peter's was built between 1791-1793 as a gift from the architect, who is buried in the Churchyard.

25. Harewood House, built 1759-1771 for Edwin Lascelles. Arthington Hall dates from 1786-1790; Farnley Hall, where the original Jacobean mansion was added to for Mr. Walter Hawksworth Fawkes. Although his Agent was a Mr. W. Wilson, Mr. Matthew Wilson of Manor House, Otley, was probably the person referred to later in the paragraph. He was of the Wilson family of Eshton and of Burley Hall, near Otley, and Deputy Lieutenant for the West Riding. Denton Park was built between 1770-1780 for Sir James Ibbotson, Bart.

26. James Carr was parish priest from 1726 to 1745; Thomas Carr followed from 1745 to 1786, when he became Headmaster of Skipton Grammar School; his son, who succeeded him, died in 1789, aged 28. The Rev. William Carr served the parish from 1789 to 1842 and the Parish Register for Bolton Abbey records that "it was this Mr. Carr that the public is indebted for the 28 miles of walks, the seats and beautiful views in Bolton Woods. 'He has worked' said Wordsworth, 'with an invisible hand of art in the very spirit of nature.'" John Umpleby not only succeeded him but assisted him in the parish and at the Boyle School for 37 years.

27. Possibly Mr. Rigg of Crossrigg Hall; a three-bay 18th century house was replaced in 1864 by Colonel Rigg who is reputed to have made his fortune in the East Indies.

28. Colgarth Park, built by Richard Watson in 1789, absentee Bishop of Llandaff, a great planter and agrarian improver.

29. Sizergh Castle, the seat of the Strickland family for centuries, is nearer to Kendall than Coniston; in Amelia mentions visiting Mr. and Mr. Strickland at Waterhead. The house visited could have been Hill Top at Winslow, a Georgian 3-bay house with spectacular views, and formerly a seat of the le Flemyng family

30. Rydal Hall, the seat of the Fleming family; the late 18th century nine-bay south front conceals the 16th century core of the house and Sir David Fleming's 17th century additions.

31. Belle Isle was designed in 1774 by John Plaw; in 1781, before it was finished, it was sold to Isabella Curwen of Workington Hall for £410. The view to Bowness was opened up when the garden was landscaped for the Curwens in 1786 by Thomas White of Retford (d. 1811). Over ten years he received £1,000 in half-yearly instalments.

32. Belmount, a neo-classical house, of 5 bays and 2½-storeys, dates from 1774. Howard Colven records that c. 1799 Carr built Belle Vue, an octagonal temple or summerhouse overlooking Lake Windermere for the Revd. William Braithwaite of Belmont, Hawkshead.

33. Ewanrigg at Wythburn was originally a pele tower; it was altered by John Christian Curwen to the design of William Heaton late in the 18th century.

34. In 1776 Joseph Pocklington built a house at Windermere; in 1778 he built, to his own design, Derwent Isle (originally Vicar's Island). Wordsworth wrote: "Mr. Pocklington, a native of Nottinghamshire ... played strange pranks by his buildings and plantations upon Vicar's Island in Derwent water, which his admiration such as it was of the country, and probably a wish to be a leader in a new fashion, had tempted him to purchase." He made his money from banking and copper and lead mining.

35. The Dalemain estate was bought in 1679 by Sir Edward Hasell, Steward to Lady Anne Clifford. His son, Edward, rebuilt the house in 1747, but the Dining Room dates from 1785.

36. Presumably they went without their second breakfast because 'to dine with Duke Humphrey' was a popular saying if one was short of money. In the 16th century itinerant beggars and debtors fearing to leave the church for fear of arrest, seeking enough to furnish a good meal, used to frequent 'Duke Humphrey's Walk' in Old St. Paul's Cathedral, which passed by a monument mistakenly believed to the tomb of Humphrey, Duke of Gloucester (1391-1447), or 'Good Duke Humphrey,' who was famous for his hospitality.

37. Drumlanrig Castle, Thornhill, is some 16 miles from Elvanfoot. It was built in the local pink sandstone between 1679 and 1691 by William Douglas, 1st Duke of Queensberry. There are superb views across Nithsdale. Another contender for the title could be Crawford Castle at Roberton.

38. Balnagowan. Vice-Admiral Sir John Lockhart Ross (1721-1790) who saw action at Quiberon Bay, assumed the name of Ross on succeeding to the Ross estate of Balnagowan in 1760.

39. The properties of Captains Nesbitt and Hamilton remain a mystery as do the men themselves. A John-More Nisbet lived at Cairnhill in Co. Lanark, while a William Ferrier-Hamilton, Lieutenant, RN, who commanded a party of sailors which dragged the cannon up the Heights of Abraham before the capture of Quebec in 1759, also seems to be linked to Cairnhill. A reference was also found to a Dunbar Hamilton, a Captain RN, born in 1766, the son of the 4th Earl of Selkirk, who died in 1796 at St. Christopher.

40. Robert Adam (1728-1792) built Mauldsley Castle, Lanarkshire, for the 5th Earl of Hyndford between 1792 and 1796.

41. Restored in the 1980s, all that now remains of Chatelherault is known as the 'Duke of Hamilton's Dog Kennels.' Alexander, 10th Duke of Hamilton (b. 1767) was Hereditary Keeper of Holyrood House. In 1810 he married Euphemia Susan, co-heiress and second daughter of William Beckford of Fonthill.

42. Was this the gothic Douglas Castle in Lanarkshire built between 1757-61 by John Adam (1721-1792) for the Duke of Douglas?

43. Lords Elphinstone of Elphinstone, Stirlingshire. John Elphinstone, the 11th Lord, was Lieutenant Governor of Edinburgh Castle.

44. Sadly no references have been found to the houses: "Mr. Marsden's, Mr. Monro's, Mr. Ship's & Others, near St. Ninians."

45. The Carron Ironworks at Larbert were established by Dr. Roebuck and Messrs. Cadell and Garbet in 1760; the guns used at the Battle of Waterloo were cast there.

46. In 1763 John Adam (1721-1792) designed offices for Sir Lawrence Dundas for Kerse (or Zetland) House, but it is not known whether they were ever built. An estimate from Carr, dated 1768, also detailed "Offices proposed to be built to the North End of the House of Kerse." The house was demolished c. 1958.

47. Mr. Forbes probably lived at Callender House.

48. The central part of Hopetoun House, which belonged to the Earls of Hopetoun, was designed by the architect Sir William Bruce in 1699, the wings being the work of William Adam.

49. For example, Dundas Castle.

50. An advertisement appeared in April 1766 inviting "Architects and others to give in plans of a New Town ..." In July 1767 Plan No. 4 by Mr. James Craig was finally accepted.

51. Several sources refer to Carr's association with the building for Sir Lawrence Dundas of Dundas House in St. Andrew's Square, now the Royal Bank of Scotland. It is suggested that "the Edinburgh Plan" for which Carr was paid £20 in 1766 might have been similar in its classical detail to Chambers' design dating from 1771; could he, in fact, have incorporated Carr's ideas, thus giving rise to the belief the York architect was involved.

52. Robert and James Adam were the architects; the foundation stone was laid in 1774. The over-life size marble statue of George III was executed in 1795 by the Hon. Mrs. Anne Seymour Damer (née Seymour-Conway), a ward and niece of Horace Walpole, who turned to sculpture when her husband, the Hon. John Damer, committed suicide in 1776.

53. The earliest statue in the city is that in Parliament Square of King Charles II, mounted and dressed as a Caeser. Said to have been imported from the continent, probably from Holland, this lead statue was supplied by James Smith, Surveyor of the King's Works.

54. Building began in 1789, Robert Adam died in 1792 and in the following year, owing to the outbreak of war, building ground to a halt; thus it was some years before the New University was completed.

55. 'Fencibles' was the name for the body of volunteer cavalry formed in 1794 for service within the United Kingdom; some 14,000 men were involved and had a stabilising effect when panic spread because of the fear of invasion.

56. Mellerstain, the home of the Earl and Countess of Haddington, was built in two stages; two wings were designed in 1725 by William Adam and the large central block by Robert Adam between 1770 and 1773.

57. Floors Castle, Kelso, the Duke of Roxburghe's seat, was designed in 1718 by Vanbrugh, William Adam was also involved, while it was later altered by Playfair.

58. Blagdon Hall was built between 1735-1740 for Matthew Ridley, a Newcastle merchant; it was remodelled in the 1780s by James Wyatt, who also built the stables and lodges. Charles Brandling built Gosforth House in 1760, using John Paine as his architect.

59. In 1791 John Carr is recorded by Colvin as having remodelled the gateway for Durham Castle for Bishop Shute Barrington

60. Vanbrugh carried out alterations at Lumley Castle for Lord Lumley, Earl of Scarbrough, after 1721.

61. In 1780 William Russell of Brancepeth purchased the Hardwick Estate from John Burdon who had been ruined by his elaborate plans for the house and garden.

62. Around 1700 Windlestone had become one of the seats of the Eden family. The present house, designed by Ignatius Bonomi, was built by Sir Robert Johnson Eden c. 1830, and cost over £40,000.

63. John Yorke of Yorke House on The Green died in 1813. The gardens were visited by Arthur Young in 1770; he wrote:"… Mr. Yorke's gardens are very well worth seeing, as the beauty of the situation is not only naturally great but much approved by art."

64. Built round a 15th century pele tower, which was given an 18th century companion. Carr made alterations and extensions at Aske c. 1765 and provided a new stable wing for Sir Lawrence Dundas who purchased the property from Lord Holderness in 1768.

65. According to a letter written in 1770 and addressed to John Grimston by Sir Robert Hildyard Bt., Carr was at that time making alterations to Sedbury Park for his son, Thornton Hildyard.

66. Extensively altered c. 1730, and again in 1790 when Thomas Atkinson added the two wings, the centre of Brough Hall is, according to Pevsner, Elizabethan.

67. Hornby Castle was the principal seat of the Conyers family until it passed to the D'Arcy family in the seventeenth century. Robert Conyers D'Arcy, 4th Earl of Holderness, died in 1778 when the earldom died also.

68. Between 1764 and 1767 John Carr made for William Danby alterations to Sir Abstrupus Danby's house of 1695-1700. At the end of the century William employed James Wyatt who added rooms to the rear of the old house.

69. A pleasure garden created from 1746 onwards by William Aislabie on the banks of the River Ure, near Grewelthorpe.

70. John Aislabie (1670-1742) was Chancellor of the Exchequer between 1714 and 1718. In 1719 he supported the South Sea Company's scheme for paying off the national debt and when it failed two years later he was expelled from the House. He returned to his estate at Studley Royal and spent his retirement refurbishing the house and laying out an elaborate pleasure garden. He was succeeded by his son, William, who bought Fountains Abbey in 1768.

71. John Carr owned the Ellenthorpe estate near Boroughbridge, and c. 1777 built Ellenthorpe Hall for his niece, Ann, and her husband. Thomas Clark, the parents of Harriet and Amelia. The family occupied the Hall until 1861.

72. The 'Mr. Hall' referred to was probably Mr. Benjamin Hall, Lord Fitzwilliam's Steward at Wentworth Woodhouse.

73. The early 15th century house had been the home of the Lister family from 1614. The 'Mr. Lister' mentioned was James, while his sisters were Martha and Anne. Probably the most famous of the family was their niece Anne: 'scholar - heiress - lesbian - traveller' who kept diaries containing 4 million words.

74. Alkrington Hall, Middleton, was designed by Giacomo Leoni in 1736; Sir Ashton Lever was High Sheriff of Lancashire, and had a museum of curiosities which he disposed of by lottery! In 1772 James Wyatt, the architect of Heaton Hall, was 26 years old; his patron, Sir Thomas Egerton (later to become the 1st Earl of Wilton) was himself only 23.

75. The term 'stuff' is used to describe woollen fabrics, but also materials not needing to be particularized. A 'muff' was a warm covering for both hands, cylindrical in shape, open at both ends, and often made of fur, while a 'tippet' was a short cape made from cloth or fur.

76. Piece Hall, according to Pevsner, was erected by Thomas Bradley in 1775 as a Cloth Market; however, Somerset House in George Street, was built by John Carr for John Royds, the banker, in 1766, and Pye Nest c. 1775 for Sir H. Edwards.

Amelia Clark's Journal
of the Tour made in the year 1796

25th July   We set out from York and went through Tadcaster and Sherbourn to
Ferrybridge. where we staid all night at Mrs. Hall's Inn, which is
pleasantly situated on the Banks of the River Aire, over which is a
handsome stone bridge with four arches.[1] On the 26th we passed
through the pretty Town of Pontefract, where are the Vestigies of a large
Castle and the remains of a beautiful Gothic Church, in our way to
Ackworth,[2] where we saw a magnificent building which was erected
about thirty years since as an appendage to the Foundling Hospital,
but that institution being reduced Two eminent Quakers, Dr. Fothergill
& Mr. Barclay, purchased the building and have made the place a
Seminary for the education of Quakers' children,[2] and when we were
there we saw three hundred boys & one hundred Girls who are Educated
and supported at only eight Guineas a year expence to their parents.

From Ackworth we proceeded to Mr. Hoyland's at Brierley[3] to
dinner, where we stayed all night, and the next day we visited Miss
Hinchliffe at Carlton, where we staid all night, and the next day we went
to New Lodge, near Barnsley, a charming house and place which belongs
to our fellow traveller, Mr. Carr.[4] Here we staid three days, and on
Sunday morning, the 31st of July, we proceeded to Wentworth House,
the magnificent seat belonging to Earl Fitzwilliam, the Front of which
extends 612 feet, in the center of which is (a) noble Portico of six
Columns, through which you enter into a magnificent hall on each side
of which are Six grand rooms, finely finished and adorn'd with paintings
& sculpture. The rooms of the Garden front consist of a noble furnish'd
Library 90 feet in length, and a Gallery 126 feet long, at one end of which
you enter into a magnificent state apartment. Besides, on this floor there
are a great number of spacious apartments & dressing rooms, and in the
chamber story above there are an amazing number of bed chambers and
dressing rooms … The chapel, in which they have prayers every night
when the family is there, is a beautiful room … The Subhall through
which you pass into the Chapel is the most singular room I ever saw;
there are forty noble Columns & pilasters in it and when it is lighted up
with the two great fires and twelve large lamps in an evening it has a very
splendid appearance.

1st August   On the first of August we visited the noble monument [designed
by Mr. Carr] Erected by Lord Fitzwilliam to the memory of his Uncle,
the Marquis of Rockingham, which stands on a charming eminence a
mile from Wentworth house. This beautiful structure is upwards of one

St. Peter's Church, Horbury

hundred feet in height; within the first story is a beautiful white marble statue[5] of the late Marquis of Rockingham in his senatorial habit upon a pedestal in the attitude of speaking; on the four sides of the pedestal there is written an Elegant Epitaph by Mr. Burke, and in the niches within the Room are place eight beautiful marble Bustos[6] ... In the second story, under a Grand triumphal Arch, there stands a large Sarcophagus supposed to contain the Ashes of the Marquis, and in (the) temple which forms the third story of the building is proposed to be placed the statue of Virtue.

From the walk round this monument you have the finest View of the environs about Wentworth house, which are grand beyond description. Through the center of this noble scenery there runs a beautiful River, the banks and every hill round which are adorn'd with the most magnificent Oak woods in the Kingdom. From this Sublime scenery we went to the noble Pyramid built by the Father of the late Marquis of Rockingham, to the top of which we ascended ninety feet high, and from which we had a very extensive view of the most beautiful country I ever beheld. At about four miles distance we had a view of the largest Column that ever was built in Europe, which was erected by the late Marquis of Rockingham ... This noble Column is distinctly seen from the Portico in the center of Wentworth house. At about one hundred & forty yards from the house the late Marquis built the most magnificent Quadrangle of Stables in this Kingdom. [The Column & Stables were design'd by Mr. Carr.] They surround a square Court ... and will hold one hundred horses, adjoining to which is a most noble Riding house 140 (feet) in length, and 45 feet wide, round which are Shops for the Blacksmiths, Joyners, Whitesmiths, Carpenters, Cabinet makers, Sadlers, Plummers & upholders, etc. who are almost constantly kept at work.

4th August   On the 4th of August we went to see Wentworth Castle, the seat of Lord Strafford, from which there is a most beautiful prospect, though different & inferior to that from Wentworth house. The West front of the house is very beautiful architecture, and the whole place is very beautifully adorn'd with woods and water which are so charmingly interspers'd as to form the most beautiful scenery, particularly from the great Gallery which is a very superb room and extends the whole length of the front of the house, in which there are a great many fine paintings. About three hundred yards from the house there stands a noble Castle[7] from the top of which you have a very extensive view of the rich surrounding Country. Here we met with a very polite reception and return'd after tea to Wentworth house, and the next day we Visited the famous Swinton pottery where we saw all the various preparation of the Clay, and which we afterwards saw converted into dishes, plates, pots and mugs & other various utensils, the operation of which is perform'd by boys and Girls and is very curious indeed, as well as ingenious & entertaining. We return'd to dinner from the pottery to our hospitable friends at Wentworth house, and the next morning we bid adieu to them. I shall long remember with pleasure this visit to Wentworth house, not only for the hospitable entertaining and the pleasant time I spent there, but for the pleasure I also enjoy'd to seeing one of the finest country's in the world and the beautiful scenes which surround this magnificant Palace.

Our next stage was to New Lodge where we dined & past the day and the next morning we went to Mr. Carr's at Wakefield[8] which is a very pretty town & beautifully situated. In the Evening we accompanied Mrs. Carr to the Theatre and were very well amused; the next day being Sunday we all went to see the new Church at Horbury, built by Mr. Carr, which is a very beautiful building; the outside … is adorn'd with three heights of columns & pilasters upon which a fluted Spire is erected, which terminates with a noble Gilt Vase. Within the steeple he has placed also, at his own expence, six new bells & a new Clock, and within the Church he has placed a noble Organ, to which they sing remarkably well. The whole inside of the Church is beautifully pew'd and the stucco work elegantly executed according to Mr. Carr's directions & at his expence, as is express'd in the Latin inscription over the outside Portico [Hanc Aedem sacram, pietatis in Deum, et amoris in solum natale monumentum, propriis sumptibus extruxit Joannes Carr architectus, 1791. Below this is written Gloria Deo in excelsis. English to the inscription: John Carr Architect built this Church at his own Expense, as a monument of his piety towards God, and of his affection to the place of his Nativity. Glory be to God on high.]

Near Horbury stands Carr Lodge, a charming house belonging to Mr. John Carr of Wakefield, the situation of which is extremely picturesque and beautiful. We staid two days more at Wakefield very agreeably, and on Wednesday, the 10th of August, we went through Leeds, which is a well built Town on the banks of the River Aire, and arrived at Otley to dinner ten miles from Leeds, in the way to which place, upon the summit of a high mountain call'd Otley Shiven there is one of the finest views in the Kingdom of the north Vale call'd Wharfdale. Lord Harewood's magnificent house, Mr. Fawkes's, Mr. Arthington's, and Sr. James Ibbotson's houses are all distinctly seen in this grand & extensive prospect. [These handsome houses were all design'd by Mr. Carr of York].

10th August   In the evening we arrived at Bolton Abbey, where we were lodged in a building exactly resembling an inchanted Castle which belongs to the duke of devonshire. We ascended to our apartments by a narrow winding stair Case, the doors of which grated upon their hinges and sounded so loud that we were terrified by their noise and appearance. The beds, however, were very good ones & we passed the night in calm repose.

11th August   The next day the Rector of the Abbey, Mr. Carr, show'd us all the beautys of this charming Vale, through which the River Wharfe rolls with great impetuosity, and is surrounded with noble woods & Lofty mountains. Upon an high hill in the Center of the Duke's park we had an extensive view of this charming scenery, in the Center of which there stands the beautiful & venerable remains of Bolton Abbey.

On our return through the park we saw an old Saxon building call'd Barden tower[9], & many beautiful 'peeps' as the Rector call'd them. On our arrival at the inchanted Castle we had a handsome dinner with a Haunch (of) Venison, also provided for us by the antique inhabitants of the Castle, to which we invited the Rector and his Sister, with whom we afterwards drank tea at the parsonage. Our antient Cook and Butler told us they had lived at the Castle almost 60 years, but the Butler's father also lived there upwards of 80 years, and he was then very well & vastly cheerful in his 98th year. Mr. Wm. Carr, the Clergyman, has got the west end of the Abbey new pewed & a new Organ put up.

From Bolton we travelled over Knaresbro' forest to Ripley to dinner and from thence, after having seen a Cotton mill in our way, we went to Studley park which is a magnificent place. Near the first entrance into this charming scenery is the cold bath; from thence you are led to the temple of Piety, which is a beautiful Dorick building with a portico before it, & from thence to a fine Gothick building, from which you have a View of the most beautiful parts of the place. We next proceeded to a Chinese Seat upon an eminence which commands the most enchanting view of Fountains Abbey, which is the most magnificent Gothick Ruin in the Kingdom. It is situated by the side of the River Skell in solemn gloom amidst hanging woods. This superb & beautiful Ruin was founded by Bishop Thurston, who was afterwards Arch Bishop of York, in 1283. At the East end there is the figure of the founder; the length of the building is 120 yards, the dining room 36 yards by 15 yards, the Cloysters are 100 yards in length & are supported by 21 pillars, above which are 21 Cells for the Monks. We saw two stone Coffins, in one of which had been the remains of Percy, Earl of Northumberland.

From this solemn scene of decay'd grandeur we went to the Banqueting house, which on the outside is a pretty rustick building, and it is very elegantly finish'd with stucco & other ornaments within, & there is an adjoining reposing room & Couch. In this charming pleasure ground are placed pretty seats to rest on, which command many very pleasing views of this enchanting scenery, at a little distance from which is (a) celebrated place call'd Michael How hill, from which you have a

Hack Fall, Grewelthorpe

very extensive view of the Vale of Mowbray, in the Center of which you see Ripon & York Cathedrals.

In this place it will be proper to mention that in the close of the last Century a piece of human antiquity existed in the neighbourhood of Fountains Abbey, still more curious than the Abbey itself, viz. that venerable instance of longevity, Henry Jenkins. Among all the Events which, in the course of one hundred and sixty nine years, had fastened upon the memory of this singular man, he spoke of nothing with such emotion as the antient state of Fountains Abbey. If he was question'd on that subject he was sure to inform you what a brave place it had once been, and would speak wih so much feeling of the clamour which its dispoilation occasioned in the Country about 150 years ago ...

From Studley we went down a beautiful Avenue with Ripon Minster in the center thereof, and spent the Evening at Ripon, which is a pretty, clean town, with a very handsome market place and an obelisk in the center thereof. The inside of the Minster has of late been very much repair'd & improved by the present dean Waddilove who shew'd us the building.

The next morning we breakfasted at six oClock and set out to see Hack Fall, a celebrated place which belongs to the Aislaby family. To describe the Grandeur & singularity of this noble scene of nature is beyond the power of my pen. Here you see hanging woods, Romantic Rocks, deep Ravines and a Rapid River rolling through the center of the scenery, which are combined together in so Romantic a manner as to produce a very astonishing Effect; in the Center of the green Terras is a handsome banquetting room, & there are several Rustick buildings erected suitable to the place from which you have different views of this magnificent scenery.

We next proceeded to Mr. danby's at Swinton to breakfast at a pretty little market town call'd Masham, in which there is a handsome Church & a Cross in the center of the market place, but in the beautiful valley near the town is a handsome Stone bridge over the River Yore. From Masham we went by Hornby Castle, the seat of the late Earl of Holderness, but now of his grandson, the Marquis of Carmarthen, eldest son of the present duke of Leeds. This noble Castle stands so Elevated as to command the whole of the Vale of Mowbray from Richmond to York.

In the evening we arrived at Caterick Bridge, an excellent Inn adjoining to the noble new stone bridge over the Rapid river Swale, near which is Brough hall, the seat of Sr. John Lawson, Baronet. The next morning, being the 14th of August, we breakfasted at Richmond after which we survey'd the romantic situation of this venerable old town, which from its dismantled Castle, which stands on the margin of the river Swale, the old Abbey and other Churches in ruins show that it has been a town of much greater consequence than it is at present. We visited Mr. York's pleasure grounds which are beautifully romantic & through which meanders the lively River swale, overhung with charming waving woods, amongst which is a handsome Gothick temple and a beautiful Gothic Menagerie.[10] In the middle of the town is a handsome market place with an ugly, new obelisk in the Center thereof. From Richmond we visited Mrs. Thistlethwaite, Miss Swann, Miss Scott & Miss Carr at Gilling, near which we saw Aske hall, the seat of Lord dundas and the ruins of Gilling castle, once the seat of the fam'd duke of Wharton.[11] We also saw Sedbury, Sr. Robt. Hildyard's seat, and we passed by a pretty place belonging to Mr. Craddock[12] in our way to Greta bridge, an excellent Inn where we breakfasted, which is very near the entrance into Mr. Morritt's beautiful park at Rookby.[13] In our way to Brough, where we staid all night, we had a view of Raby Castle,[14] the noble seat of the Earl of darlington, and in our road, we also saw Barnard Castle and town, and the noble bridge which spans in one Arch the whole River Tees, design'd by Mr. Carr.[15]

From Brough we went to appleby in Westmorland which is charmingly situated on the banks of the River Eden; the Castle, which stands at one end of the Town, has a very Romantic appearance with its towers & battlements rising through the surrounding woods.

On our way to Penrith in Cumberland we were introduced, by a letter from Mrs. Thistlethwaite, to Mrs. Atkinson at Temple Sowerby, who very politely show'd us such a collection of beautiful shells from almost every part of the Globe as is not to be seen in any other part of the Kingdom. About one oClock we reached Penrith where we staid all night. The town is prettily situated near which is Carleton,[16] the seat of the late Lawyer Wallace, the scenery round which is very beautiful by the Conflux of the Rivers Lowther & Eamont & the View of Broome Hall[17] and Castle and the surrounding woods; the Church at Penrith is a handsome building, the gallerys of which are supported by Red stone pillars.

Early in the morning we set out for Poolley bridge to breakfast, the way to which place through the charming Vale of Eamont is beautiful beyond description. We passed by delamain, a large Red stone house belonging to Mr. Hassels, & Hutton St. John & an old mansion of Mr. Huddleston's[18] in our way to the noble lake call'd Ulswater, to have an advantageous view of which we attempted to ascend to the summit of a Grand mountain which is covered with wood call'd Dun Mallet, but we were not able, from fatigue, to reach the top of the mountain. We however ascended to such a height that we had a very extensive view of this grand Lake which is nine miles in length & a mile at least in breadth, at one end of which lived not long ago, one Parson Mattison, who having a few

Acres of land of his own was call'd the King of Patterdale & was Minister of the place sixty years & lately died at the age of ninety ...

From Ulswater we proceeded by Dacre Castle towards the high mountains call'd Saddle back and Leadpot, alongside of which we went to Keswick. After dinner we Cross'd a part of the grand Lake of Derwentwater towards Pocklington Island where we landed and were permitted to see Mr. Pocklington's house, from the windows of which you have a view of the whole of this transparent lake and the surrounding mountains call'd Borrowdale fells, which are covered with wood and render the scenery extremely picturesque and beautiful. We sail'd round the lake to see the grand cascade call'd Lowdore fall, & from which place you have a view of Basingthwaite water which is skirted with Wood on one side thereof, and the noble mountain, Skiddaw, bounds the other side of this beautiful lake.

In the evening we visited Mr. Crosthwaite's Museum, and early the next morning we left Keswick and went along the sweet Vale of St. John to Wythburn to breakfast; the road runs along the bottom of this charming Vale by the sides of Grassmeer and Thirlmeer, two beautiful lakes which are surrounded with magnificent mountains. Here you see Falcon Crag, Castle head and Lion's Cliff, the tops of which rise into the Clouds, & down their sides pour Cataracts of water to supply the lakes below; but above all the rest, rise in Majestic grandeur, Cachidecam & Helvellyn, at the foot of which we breakfasted, and were told that it was full four miles to the summit of Helvellyn. We then proceeded to Rydale Hall, over Dunmaile raise, the seat of Sr. Michael Fleming, in which park are two beautiful Cascades, one of which falls an immense height from an high rock, the other, through a rude Arch of a bridge which indeed is extremely beautiful & picturesque, from the Grotto in the Garden.

From Rydale we went by Ambleside & Clapper gate & by Mrs. Pritchard's to Keensground, near Hawkshead, to Mr. & Mrs. Riggs, where we met with a hearty welcome & with whom we staid a week. The day following we spent with Mr. & Mrs. Strickland at Waterhead, whose house is situated at one end of the Grand lake call'd Coniston water ... This lake is surrounded by exceeding high mountains call'd Coniston fells, in which the fine Blue slate is got & which is convey'd in small Vessels down the Lake to Pennybridge & there shipp'd to every part of the Kingdom.

The next day we Visited the magnificent Lake call'd Windermeer, which is only five miles from Hawkshead, a very beautiful road along the side of Easthead lake. On our arrival on this margin of this noble lake of Windermeer we ascended to the summit of a high mountain near the ferry house from which we had a view of almost the whole extent of this

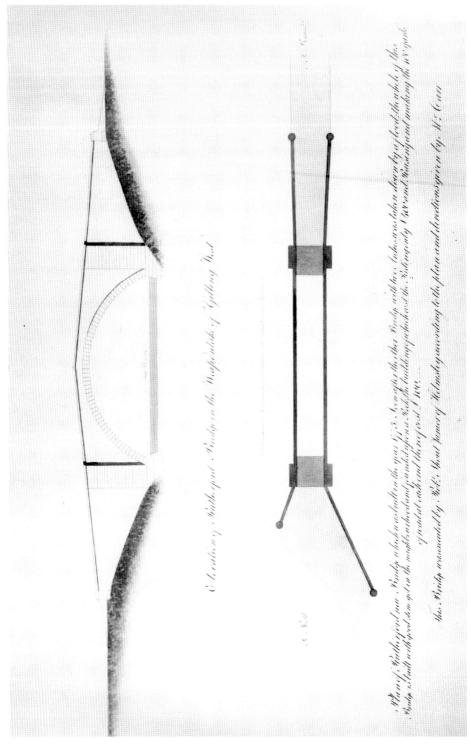

Rutherford Bridge

42

magnificent lake & the surrounding mountains … This astonishing View exceeded in sublimity and variety everything we had before seen.

At our arrival at the Ferry house we cross'd a part of the Lake to visit Mr. & Mrs. Curwen with whom Mr. Carr was intimately acquainted. They live upon the Island in the middle of the lake which is beautifull planted & laid out. We were politely received and invited to dine with them the next day to see a grand sailing match upon the lake, which we accepted, and spent a very pleasant day with them, and in the evening by Moonlight we were ferryed over the lake by young Mr. Curwen, and arrived safely again at our good friends' house at Keensground.

On Sunday Mr. Carr left us to go to Mr. Curwen's house at Workington, near Whitehaven; we went to Hawkshead Church with Mrs. Rigg, and on Monday we went to Mr. Braithwaite's, the Clergyman who has a handsome modern house at Bellmont, from which we had a charming view of the beautiful Lake & its environs call'd Easthead water. On Tuesday Mr. Carr return'd and on Wednesday we set out for Holker, the seat of Lord Frederick Cavendish,[19] who is Uncle of the present Duke of Devonshire.

The whole ride from Hawkshead is 18 miles, the greatest part of which is close to the side of Windemeer Lake and is beautiful beyond description. Mr. Sands' place[20] at Graithwait is vastly pretty on the road, and Mr. Rawlinson's house and gardens[21] stand near the lake and adorn the road very much. Sir John Legard[22] & Mr. Dixon[23] have also very pretty houses on the opposite side of the Lake, and about Newby Bridge, at the foot of the Lake, the country is vastly picturesque & beautiful all the way to Cartmel. We arrived at Holker to dinner, where we also met Lord John Cavendish, who, after dinner, very politely walk'd round the park with us to show us the place and the charming views of the Sea. In the house there (were) a great many fine paintings by Claud Lorrain and Canaletti, and a beautiful picture of Vandyke painted by himself, who is a handsome man with flaxen colour'd hair, a fine picture of St. Francis by Correggio, and a great many charming family pictures.

25th August On Thursday, the 25th, we set out in Lord Frederick's Carriage to cross the ten mile sands to Lancaster, and happy it was for us that he was so polite as to send us in his chaise, for in crossing the two rapid Rivers, the Kent and Kere, we should have been prettily soused as they were not less than a mile in breadth & a considerable depth. We heard many dreadful storys of persons being lost in crossing these sands, but the Guide who conducted us over the rivers told us that very few people were lost. His Father and Grandfather, he said, were drown'd but they were not lost, for they found them again. We, however, arrived safe at Lancaster at Billy Kew's about twelve oClock, a dirty Inn but very Civil people, where we ate a hearty dinner, after which we went to see the

Buxton

44

noble Castle, built by John of Gaunt, in which are being built the new courts of Justice. From the Churchyard there is one of the finest views in England of the noble River Lune running into the Sea, and the magnificent hills call'd Hard Knot, and wry nose, Wallow Grag & Cawsey grand Pike. We also saw the handsome new Bridge with five Arches and the Aqueduct over the River Lune which cost upwards of forty thousands, over which a navigation is making from Wigan in Lancashire to Kendal in Westmorland.

The next morning we had a wet ride to Garstang to our breakfast, after which we went to Preston to dinner, and took our Tea with Mr. Riggs' Sister, who very politely walk'd out with us to see the charming views upon the River Ribble near the Town. The next morning we went to Chorley to breakfast & afterwards to Manchester to dinner. The assembly rooms here are very handsome & we saw a handsome new Church, the noble Infirmary and many other very spacious buildings, but Mr. Lever's handkerchief manufactory is an astonishing sight. He supplys the whole continent of America with handkerchiefs and many other parts of Europe. The Cotton manufactory is carried on at this place to vast extent.[24] The town is very large & the new streets are wide & well laid out in straight lines.

We next proceeded upon a rough pavement to Stockport in Cheshire to breakfast, and from thence we reach'd Buxton to dinner, which was so full of company we had great difficulty to obtain a bed. The semi-circular building at this place is the Grandest Fabrick I had ever seen; it is called the Crescent, the architecture of which is very beautiful, being adorn'd with fluted Columns & pilasters upon a Rusticated Arcade, under which all the company walk. We were much astonish'd with the Baths, the water in which seem'd smoking hot, of which in the morning the company drink copiously, and walk about under the Arcade. The assembly room is 80 feet long, 30 feet wide and 30 feet height, the whole of which is very elegantly furnish'd, and adorn'd with Glasses & Lustres, but the stables are the most singular building in the Kingdom. The outside thereof is Octangular and the inside is a Circle of 180 feet in diameter, supported by a noble Colonnade under which the company ride in rainy weather, and they may, if they please, ride twenty miles under cover. These Stables hold 120 horses & they are built, like the Crescent, with very fine Stone. The Colonade under which the company ride is 28 feet high and is the finest thing in Europe. The high Mountains and deep ravines which surround this place are very singular & Romantic.

After dinner we left this singular place & proceeded to Chatsworth that Evening … Chatsworth house is situated in a delightful Vale and is a magnificent Building, within the center of which is a noble court adorn'd with Colonades. The West front towards the River is very beautiful architecture, with Columns in the center part and pilasters on each side thereof. The principal entrance is through a noble painted hall, at the end of which you ascend into the principal story by a double flight of steps into a beautiful drawing room, Music room, dining room, & a Grand Gallery. The Chapel is also a beautiful Room, the lower part of which & the Tribune is wainscotted with Cedar, and the upper part & Ceiling is finely painted by Vario, representing the miracles of our Saviour. At one end is a grand marble Altar piece adorn'd with Corinthian columns, upon which are two beautiful marble statues representing Hope and Charity.

From this floor you ascend up a magnificent Stair Case into the grandest suite of apartments I ever beheld, some of which are hung with rich Tapestry, others with fine Oak wainscott & rich Carving, & all the ceilings are beautifully painted by the celebrated Vario, & there (are) a great many other Charming pictures by the most esteem'd masters. The bedrooms and beds are very Antique & Grand, particularly in the apartment in which the unfortunate Queen of Scots was confined. The walls of the great Stair Case are finely painted & all the panels in the great gallery are beautifully painted with the story from pastor Fido.[25] At one end of the great hall is finely painted by Vario the inside of the senate house at Rome with a representation of the death of Julius Caesar stabb'd by Brutus. The walls on each side thereof are painted with Roman Triumphs & Victorys; the floor is laid with marble & the niches and stairs are adorn'd with Golden Vases and gilt ornaments.

The surrounding park & pleasure grounds are equal in grandeur & beauty to the inside of the house ... The Gardener play'd the whole of the water works for our amusement, during which a great many country people from a neighbouring fete came to see the water works who, being dispersed among the artificial trees, got woefully soused with the water pouring down upon them from the unsuspected branches. Through the Center of the park the beautiful River derwent is seen from the South & West points of the house, over which is a handsome bridge of three arches. The park rises in majestic Grandeur above the River, and is finely adorn'd with noble masses of wood, scattered herds of Cattle & beautiful deer, one end of which terminates with a terrific scene of tremendous, huge rocks & the other end thereof extends to the beautiful vale call'd darley dale. We ascended through the woods to a building call'd The Stand, from which we had a noble view of the Country which for variety of hills, dales, Rocks & woods exceeded any views I had ever seen.

Our reception & entertainment in this noble palace was comfortable beyond expression, and made our stay here very delightful, & for our amusement there were musical instruments in almost every room below stairs ...

2nd September   From Chatsworth we set out on the 2nd September and
proceeded through darley dale along the beautiful banks of the derwent
to the Bridge near matlock, over which is the first grand specimen of
what we were to expect; as we advanced towards the boat house the views
became more interesting & soon after the great Torr appeared which is a
magnificent rock decorated with wood & stain'd with various hues,
yellow, Green & Grey. On the opposite side the Rocks contracting the
road slope diagonally; these straits open into the vale of Matlock, a
romantic and most delightful scene, in which the Ideas of sublimity
and beauty are blended in a very high degree from the combin'd Effect
of hanging woods, stupendious Rocks and the rapid river running
through the bottom of this deep ravine, which extends about two
miles in length & is not more than half a mile in breadth. The grand
rampart opposite to the principal Torr is beautifully shaded with woods
which grow among the Rocks and Garnish the Cliffs, and by admitting
the light and shade give an airiness to the scene. The river derwent
which winds under this semicircular screen is a broken, rapid stream,
delving among the Rocks & woody projections, and is only heard
but not seen; indeed, the whole of this singular scenery is sublime &
wonderful; not only the Eye is pleased but the imagination is filled.
This charming Valley terminates with a view of Mr. Arkwright's Gothick
house, his cotton Mills and a little church which he has built for his
workmen.

Our next Stage was to Wirksworth where we breakfasted and from
then to the Inn at Kedleston near Lord Scarsdale's, whose Magnificent
house[26] we visited the next morning, and were very politely received by
the housekeeper, who presented us with fruit & Cake. The entrance into
the house is by a noble hall, 67 feet by 42 feet, which is adorn'd with
twenty beautiful Corinthian Columns of Staffordshire marble; the whole
is lighted by three Skylights. On each side of the hall is the dining room
& beautiful breakfast room, each 36 by 24 feet, & the drawing room is 58
by 28 feet & the Library 36 x 24 (feet), adjoined to which is a beautiful
round room, 42 feet (in) diameter, which is call'd the Saloon & is lighted
by a Skylight; adjoining … is a handsome bedchamber & two dressing
rooms. In the library is a fine picture by Rembrandt which represents the
Interpretation of Balshazzer's dream, a Charming holy family, some
good heads, one of Shakespear by Vandyck, and Andromache chain'd to
the Rock. In the drawing room, the death of Abel and the Last Supper
are two grand pictures by Luti, and the woman of Samaria & St. John
preaching in the wilderness are charming pictures by Coypt. In the
breakfast room is another holy family and the flight into Egypt - very fine
pictures, and there are a great many beautiful pictures in several other
rooms. The outside architecture & inside finishing of this house is very

grand & beautiful, and the situation thereof is charmingly adorn'd with Wood and water.

We next proceeded to Derby where we saw the beautiful Porcelain manufactory,[27] and the Elegant white China figures which are equal to any french China that ever was made. We next went to Burton-on-Trent where we dined and staid all night at a dirty Inn and a dirty town, where they brew fine Ale & send it to every part of Europe, but we did not taste it as we found the wine pretty good.

The next morning we set out at six oClock and arrived at Litchfield at nine, where we got a second breakfast, after which we visited the Cathedral which is a very beautiful Gothick building and has lately been cleaned in the inside & the outside very much repaired. There is a handsome monument to the memory of Garrick and another to the memory of Doctor Johnson, and a very handsome one also to the memory of Lady Mary Wortley Montague. Over the altar table is a beautiful painted window by Jarvis of the ascension of Our Saviour.[28] On the outside of the west end are statues of all the Kings of Judea in niches. The whole building is very elegant Gothic, but is very much smaller than York Minster.

We next proceeded to Birmingham to a late dinner, and the next morning we walked round the Town and saw a curious whip manufactory and Clay's curious Tea board manufactory.[29] The streets are wide & handsome and very well built and there are several handsome Churches.

Our next stage was to Broomsgrove where we dined, and in the Evening arrived at Worcester which is a pretty town with one very spacious long street through it, many handsome shops and a noble town hall and an antient Saxon Cathedral.

From Worcester we went to Glocester where we saw a very noble Cathedral, part Saxon & Gothick architecture with fine Cloysters. Here we saw a very curious pin manufactory, which imploys a great many people, chiefly children.[30]

We next cross'd the Severn into Wales & went to Monmouth & Ross, where we breakfasted at the house of the Man of Ross, and afterwards went along the banks of the charming River Wye to Chepstow and Pearsefield; the views along the banks of the Wye are esteem'd the most beautiful & picturesque of any in England, but I think they are not so noble & beautiful as the banks of Easthead water, and Windermeer from Hawkshead to Newby Bridge near Cartmel. The road from Monmouth to Chepstow is very mountainous with many noble views; particularly at two miles distance from Chepstow there is the most extensive and animated view in the Kingdom. You see distinctly into thirteen countys, through the Center of which the sublime Severn Rolls with Majestic grandeur. Chepstow Castle, with its Gothick towers & broken Embrasures covered with Ivy, and the Bridge over the Wye, are beautifully picturesque in the foreground of this magnificent view.

After dinner we cross'd the River Wye and ascended to the summit of a high mountain, from which we had a delightful view of the conflux of the Wye with the Severn, and the vessels in full sail upon both Rivers, for here the tide flows 60 feet high under Chepstow bridge, the Rocky banks of which & windings of the stream are very singular and beautiful.

The next morning we set out in a Chaise and went to the celebrated station call'd Wine Cliff, in order to have the finest view of that charming place call'd Piersefield, lately the property of Col. Morris & Mr. Smith, but now Col. Woods.[31] The beautys of Piersefield arise from the combin'd Effect of the noble hanging woods & stupendous Rocks on each side of the River Wye and its conflux with the Severn, which noble river is distinctly seen for 20 miles to Bristol. From this Grand & delightful scenery we proceeded towards Tintern abbey, the way to which is down a deep Ravine through hanging woods & so narrow a path Two carriages cannot meet. The descent through this solemn, Gloomy Glen extends three miles before you come in sight of the Venerable Abbey, the situation of which, near the banks of the Wye, is solemn & singular beyond description. The surrounding Rocks & hanging woods rise on every side as high as the fabrick, the walls of which and its broken towers & pinnacles are covered with Ivy & produce a very singular & beautiful appearance. The East and West end windows are very beautiful and intire, & many other parts thereof are very beautiful architecture. The building was founded in 1131 by Walter de Clare & dedicated to St. Mary. Around this beautiful building are a few scattered huts, out of which there came many curious, antique figures of Welsh Men & Women who seem'd almost Coeval with the Abbey & were astonish'd at the sight of us & our carriage, & there were many little Tivils of Boys & Girls also who stared astonishingly.

We had great difficulty in ascending through the rugged Ravine again, on each side of which are several deep and dangerous precipices, but we were amply recompens'd on our reaching the summit by the enchanting View which we had again of Pearsefield & the charming surrounding Country. In all our travels we had seen no view which exceeded the beauty & sublimity of the scene before us, and which we were told exceeded by much every other part of Wales. We therefore, in the Evening, crossed the sublime Severn, with a charming Gale of wind, in about an hour at the new passage and staid all night at the Bank house.

At six oClock the next morning we set out for Bristol and in our way thither we stopp'd at the hot wells[32] & breakfasted to taste the water and see the place, which from the noble Rocks and hanging woods, with the River Avon running through the middle of them, very much resembles Matlock, & the town is increased in buildings to a vast extent and it is really a beautiful Romantic place & the Country round it is very bold & animated. From this place to Bristol is two miles & it is now built all the way. We passed through Bristol to Bath,[33] which is a charming Country and arrived there to dinner at the White Lion Inn, after which we procured lodgings in Pierrepont street, at Mrs. Petrie's, betwixt the South & North parades. This noble City is situated low on the banks of the River Avon, the surrounding hills on every side are very high and very beautiful. On the North side are three beautiful Crescents, one of which is call'd the New Crescent, another Landsdown Crescent, and Cambden Place, all very handsome buildings, but the Circus exceeds them all in beautiful Architecture. The streets are, in general, well built & very regular, particularly Pultney Street, which leads to the publick Gardens, into the entrance of which you pay sixpence & for sixpence more you have tea. The whole Ground is prettily laid out and you may amuse yourself in the Labyrinth and Merlin's Swings (for) as long as you please.

Queen's square is a beautiful part of the town & is surrounded with very handsome, regular buildings & an Elegant Church. Gay street joins this square and leads into the Circus, above mentioned, which forms one great Circle of buildings of equal height, with three orders of Columns, Viz. the Dorick, Ionick and Corinthian. There are many handsome Churches & Chapels & a noble Gothic Cathedral call'd the Abbey, near which is the Pump room, where all the company assemble every morning to drink the water, and it is really very entertaining to see the Variety of Gay and Grotesque figures strutting about the Room. It is singular & curious to see the Ladies & Gentlemen from the windows of the Pump Room all bathing together. We were astonish'd at the sight.

The old Assembly Rooms are near the Parades and are handsome, the dancing room 90 feet by 36 and 34 feet high. The new Assembly room and the Card rooms are esteem'd the handsomest in England. The dancing room is 106 feet by 43, and 40 feet high. The Card rooms are also very elegantly fitted up, betwixt which is a handsome Octangular Anti room.

There is another handsome square call'd St. James square, but the Parades are the most pleasant part of the City, & most convenient for infirm people as they are near the Pump room, & being all finely flagg'd no Coaches are suffered to pass upon them. They have also a charming View of the surrounding country, & of that noble place call'd Prior Park which was built by the late Mr. Allan.

During the time we were at Bath there was a very Grand exhibition of Fireworks which we had the pleasure of seeing in spring gardens. We staid a week in this noble City, where we spent our time very agreeably in a party of very good company at the same house where we lodged.

We next proceeded to Frome in Somersetshire, on the River Frome, over which is a large stone bridge. The whole town is full of clothmakers. Here we spent the Evening and early next morning we set out for Mr. Hoare's at Stourhead, in the way to which place we call'd to see Longleat,[34] a noble house belonging to the Marquis of Bath, built in the reign of Queen Elizabeth. The park is delightful & extensive, full of fine deer and a noble, river-like piece of water runs by the house, which is an immense fabrick & contains a great many fine rooms & paintings, a great many family pictures by Holbein, and one celebrated picture of Jane Shaw, and two of Mary, Queen of Scots. The Hall is hung round with fine hunting & hawking pictures; large stags' horns fly in a curious manner.

We breakfasted at Maiden Bradley and from thence it is only two miles to Mr. Hoare's,[35] which is one of the most delightful places we had seen. Every room is full of the most charming pictures; the picture of Elisha and the dead child by Rembrandt, is wonderfully executed; the wise men bringing presents to our Saviour, the Rape of the Sabines, Cleopatra taken Prisoner by Augustus Caesar, Penelope awaking on the return of Ulysses, are Esteem'd capital pictures. There are also several fine Madonas, John the baptist's head, and an infinite number of beautiful Landscapes. The Saloon is a handsome room of 50 feet by 30, and 30 (feet) high, the whole of which is filled with the most beautiful paintings. We were highly delighted with this charming house and its beautiful situation & pleasure grounds, which extend three miles before you arrive at the noble triangular building, erected by the late Mr. Hoare, the banker, in memory of King Alfred the great, upon the place where he defeated the Danes.[36] We ascended to this high tower from which we had a view of the Mendip Hills and a beautiful surrounding Country. There is a noble statue of King Alfred placed in a Nich above the door into the Tower. The pleasure grounds & woods, and the noble Lake which runs through the valley before the house, are very extensive & beautiful, & on an eminence is built an elegant Rotunda in the form of the Sybil's temple at Tivoli in italy, which has a fine Effect.

From this charming place we went ten miles over the Wiltshire Downs to a small market town call'd Hindon and staid all night, and early in the morning we proceeded to Fonthill,[37] the celebrated seat of the late Alderman Beckford, who was twice Lord Mayor of London. The house was burn(ed) down when it was nearly finished in 1755, but is now rebuilt in a more magnificent manner. In the Center of the house is a noble Portico, and the wings are connected by an elegant Colonade; the inside of the house is superbly finish'd and furnish'd, particularly the Base Story, the ceilings in which are finely Gilt, and the walls hung with

The principal Front of Basildon House in Berkshire

This is one of the houses of John Brown

J. Brown of York Archt.

Scale of Feet

London April 10. 1768 Engraved & Published by George Richardson.

Basildon

damasks the same as the Turkish Sofas. There is a handsome Gallery, filled with fine pictures & a marble Statue of the late Alderman. The situation of Fonthill is more beautiful than any place we had seen; the woods on every hill are magnificent and the water in front of the house and along the valley is beautiful.

From this place we went to debtford Inn to our second breakfast, and from then over Salisbury plains to see the famous druids' Temple call'd Stonehenge, which is the most astonishing work of British antiquity in the kingdom & is supposed to have been a place of worship. The fabrick is of a circular form composed with 120 huge stones, about 22 feet in height above ground, some of them 8 feet broad & 4 feet 6 inches thick, and about 6 feet under. These form the outer circle, upon the tops of which are laid large, massive stones mortised down upon the heads of the upright stones. Within this great circle is another, inner circle composed of smaller stones, in the center of which there are the remains of an altar on which the Priests, or druids as they were call'd, exhibited their sacrifices and perform'd their religious ceremonys. This magnificent structure is rendered more astonishing from its not being known from whence the stones were got, or how they could be brought to the place, as there are no stones of such magnitude in the County.

The distance from the remains of this sacred temple to Salisbury is about ten miles over the downs, upon which we saw the remains of a noble Roman encampment, & a great many of various sized Timuli or round hills of earth which evidently indicate that a battle must have been fought upon these plains as the remains of a Human body are always found within those round hills and, according to the dignity of the person, the hills are raised higher or lower.

We arrived at Salisbury about four oClock, the whole town in a bustle in consequence of the king having just pass'd through. The next day, being Sunday, we went to the Cathedral Church where we heard a good sermon and saw Bishop douglas and dean Evans, after which we view'd the internal parts of this beautiful structure. Over the alter there is a beautiful painted window of the ascension of our Saviour; the Gothick pillars which support the Roof and Spire are remarkably slender but the aisles are narrow & it is not so beautiful within as Litchfield Cathedral. The Spire is remarkably high & handsome, and has been Erected some time after the body of the Church as the Architecture thereof is the most elegant Gothick composition, but the body of the Church is a mixture of the Saxon kind of Gothick.[38]

The Area round this Cathedral is very ample & spacious & prettily laid out with walks to which the polite people of the town resort in an Evening. The Bishop's palace & prependal houses surround this Area. This town of Salisbury, or Sarum, has nothing remarkable in it except

Basildon Park

the Cathedral & two other Churches. The Market place is spacious & there is a pretty-looking town hall. The wild downs which surround this City are very extensive & chiefly pastured with long legg'd sheep, the wool of which is short & fine & very proper for the fine Cloth manufacturers about Frome.

We visited Lord Pembroke's at Wilton[39] from Salisbury, which is a magnificent old house round a Court, every room in which abounds with more Statues & Bustos than any other house in England, and there (are) also a great many charming pictures, particularly the painting of the Pembroke family by Vandyke. The Woman of Samaria by Guiseppi, the holy family by Gennari, a great many beautiful marble tables, one of which is composed of one hundred & thirty five different specimens of agates & marbles, and a curious Groupe of eleven figures. There is a beautiful Busto of marble of Marcia, the wife of Septimus Severus, another fine one of Brutus who Kill'd Caesar, and Antinuous, the favourite of the Roman Emperor, Hadrian.

The next day we went to Andover, to our second breakfast, where Mr. Carr met with two Gentlemen of his acquaintance who were come to dine there, a Mr. Cox and Mr. Lethulier,[40] who live in the neighbourhood. Mr. Cox would gladly have had us gone home with him for a few days, but we proceeded on to Newbury in Berkshire, which is a large, handsome Town, a handsome Town hall & dancing room with two good pictures in it.

In the morning we went across Country road to Sr. Francis Sykes at Basildon[41] in Berkshire; the Roads were bad beyond description for ten miles. On our arrival we were exceeding politely received by Sr. Francis, Lady Sykes, and their lovely daughter, and with whom we spent a very pleasant week. The situation of the house and the surrounding Country are extremely beautiful; every hill is covered with noble beech woods, and the River Thames runs through the meadows in Front of the house, the entrance into which is very singular and beautiful. [The house was designed by Mr. Carr]. You ascend into the principal story by a double flight of steps under a beautiful Loggio of Columns; the Hall is 36 feet by 24, The dining room 40 by 24, the drawing room an Octagon of 36 feet diameter, the Library 32 by 24, (the) Breakfast room 30 by 26, and on the same floor is a noble bed chamber & two dressing rooms. The offices or wings are united to the house by a Corridor, & the whole is united to form one uniform and elegant front. Lady Sykes took us to Reading fair, where we saw more than ten thousand pounds worth of fine cheese, and we jaunted about somewhere or other every day.

From this charming place we next proceeded to Fawley Court,[42] the seat of Strickland Freeman, Esqr., a particular friend of Mr. Carr's. Here we spent five days very pleasantly indeed, as Mrs. Freeman is a charming person, and they had some very pleasant company with them. The house is a very magnificent one, & situated on the banks of the Thames near Henley. In his noble Riding house, Mr. Freeman has a great many beautiful Manege horses which he rides every morning, the docility and actions of which are very curious to see. They have a charming Summer house on an Island in the Thames to which we sail'd, and we went to see a charming place which lately belong'd to General Conway, now to Lord Malmsbury.[43] The Garden & pleasure grounds are extremely beautiful, particularly the noble Terras which has an extensive view of the Thames & the surrounding Beech woods with which this country abounds.

1st October   On Saturday, the first of October, we set out for Oxford and arrived there to dinner at the Bear in the middle of the high street, after which we visited Christ's Colledge, the beautiful Peckwater court, and the noble hall & Library belonging to this superb Colledge, built by Cardinal Woolsey; the hall is 115 feet long, 40 wide & 50 high, the sides of which are adorn'd with charming paintings, particularly the late Lord Primate of Ireland, Dr. Robinson, & the present Archbishop of York, Dr. Markham.[44] I shall not attempt to enumerate the several noble Colledges and Churches which adorn this Venerable City, the seeing of which gave us inexpressible pleasure, and I am told this City has more the appearance & Grandeur of Rome than any other place in England.

We went to the university Church on Sunday morning and were surprised to hear nothing there but a short Sermon. We therefore immediately set out and went to the duke of Marlborough's at Blenheim,[45] and on our alighting at Woodstock were told that the house is never shown on a Sunday. Mr. Carr, however, wrote to the duke to desire he would permit us to see the house, along with some foreigners that were there, and he very politely gave us leave to see the whole inside of this magnificent palace. Every room abounds with charming pictures by the most celebrated Masters, and you see worked in rich & beautiful Tapestry all the duke of Marlborough's battles. The library is a very large & finely furnish'd room, and in the adjoining chapel is a superb monument to the memory of the great duke of Marlborough. The pleasure grounds & park is very beautiful and extensive. The Bridge, and noble Lake of water which fills the valley in front of the house, are truly noble and Magnificent.

In the Evening we return'd to Oxford and from thence we proceeded, the day following, towards London, on our way to which place we visited the Marchioness of Rockingham at Hillenden house,[46] near Uxbridge, where we spent two days with her Ladyship and Lady Charlotte Wentworth, the late Marquis of Rockingham's Sister. We breakfasted at ten, half-dined at one, and at Seven we dined with her Ladyship very Elegantly, drunk Tea at Eleven and went to bed when we pleased.

From this charming place we went through Uxbridge to London, and on our way thither we took an early dinner at a Village at a few miles distance from Town and arrived there about three oClock in the afternoon, in Prince's street, Hanover square, where we staid only three or four days, after which we removed into old Burlington street, where we were receiv'd in the most friendly manner by Mr. and Mrs. Harvey, they being particular friends of my Uncle Carr's, & during the time we staid in London they paid us every kind attention. It would be impossible to give an account of every thing we saw in London; we Visited, however, that we thought worthy of our notice, viz. St. Paul's, Westminster Abbey, The Panorama,[47] Levers' Museum,[48] The Tower, Astly's Amphitheatre,[49] and were taken to the Theatres by Lady and Miss Sykes, our Basildon friends, who often visited us and politely entertain'd us during our three weeks' stay in Town.

On our leaving this Magnificent City, we proceeded towards Cambridge through Ware to Wade's Mill, where we spent the Evening, and the next day we arrived at The Rose Inn in the market place in Cambridge. The next day we visited all the principal buildings and Colledges. We particularly admired King's Colledge Chapel, as it is esteem'd one of the most beautiful Gothick buildings in Europe, the ceiling of which is stone and adorn'd with the most beautiful Gothick compartments. Trinity Colledge consists of two noble Quadrangular Courts, and is, I think, equal in magnitude and magnificence to any Colledge in Oxford; the Arcades in the second court are very handsome, and the Library, design'd by Sr. Chrisr. Wren, is a noble room, 160 feet in length, and the breadth and height thereof are each 40 feet. Clare Hall is also a beautiful Colledge and very uniformly built. The publick walks behind these colledges are very beautiful & convenient for the Students to walk in along the banks of the River Cam, over which are several handsome bridges. The Senate house is a very beautiful building, the outside of which is adorn'd with noble Corinthian Columns & pilasters in the Grecian manner, and the inside thereof is finely finish'd with Oak wainscott & projecting Gallerys for the Audience. The situation and general appearance of Cambridge is much inferior to Oxford, as well as the Colledges & public buildings, except those above mentioned.

From Cambridge we proceeded next to Huntingdon along a charming road through very large cornfields. At Huntingdon we staid all night, and the next night we spent at Wandsford in England, and from Wandsford we went to Lord Exeter's at Burleigh, near Stamford, which is a magnificent place; the house was built by the Lord Chancellor

Newark Town Hall

Burleigh in the time of Queen Elizabeth. All the principal rooms in this noble house are adorn'd with fine pictures & done by the most celebrated painters; the Park is grand and spacious and the Avenues are formed with venerable old trees, through which you see a beautiful serpentine piece of water. The Steward & housekeeper, whom we had seen at Chatsworth, entertain'd us with very great Civility and hospitality.

The next Evening we slept at Post Witham, and the next morning we breakfasted at Grantham and view'd the handsome Church and Market place, and from thence we proceeded to Newark where we staid all night. At this place there is a handsome Church and a very Elegant Town Hall, design'd by my Uncle Carr,[50] in the Center of one side of the spacious Market place.

4th November   The next day we reach'd Doncaster where we spent the Evening, and the day after we arrived at my Uncle Carr's at Wakefield, viz. on the 5th of November, where we remain'd three weeks and spent our time in a very agreeable manner indeed, Wakefield being a very gay town, and charmingly situated; the whole country around it is very beautiful.

28th November   From this place we set out for York, where we arrived on the 28th of November, after having been absent from thence upwards of four months, and in that time we travelled almost three thousand miles.

Footnotes - 1796

1. The bridge at Ferrybridge was built by J.C. and John Watson in 1765.
2. Ackworth was built in 1758, bought by Dr. John Fothergill in 1778 and opened as a school in 1779.
3. Mr. Hoyland's house at Brierley was possibly the pre-Reformation Brierley Manor.
4. New Lodge at Barnsley belonged to John Carr but was occupied by his nephew, John Clark.
5. The statue of the Marquis of Rockingham was carved by Sir Joseph Nollekens c. 1782.
6. The pedestal on which the statue stands and those in the alcoves were supplied by the Fishers of York. The bill for the 218 dozen capital letters carved for the epitaph and the pedestals amounted to £211.10s. 0d. and included £8 for the hire of a horse and cart.
7. Stainbrough Castle, a Gothic folly built by the 1st Earl of Strafford in 1739.
8. Carr Lodge, Horbury, originally called 'Sun Royd', which was built c. 1765 by Joseph Bayldon and bought by John Carr in 1789 for his nephew John Carr, an attorney.
9. Built with Gothic details in the late 16th century for Lord Clifford and restored by Lady Anne Clifford c. 1658-9.
10. Temple Lodge in the grounds of The Green, Richmond, was built in 1769 as a menagerie.
11. Philip, Duke of Wharton (1698-1731) was son and heir of Thomas Wharton, Marquis of Wharton (1648-1715). Philip was President of the 'Hell Fire Club', he dissipated his estates and sold his paintings to Sir Robert Walpole, including several Van Dycks and Lelys, while his Westmorland estates were sold to Sir Robert Lowther. Alexander Pope wrote of him as being 'from no vice exempt.'

12. Could this have been Carlton Hall, Aldbrough St. John?

13. c. 1776 Carr was almost certainly responsible both for the stables and for internal work at Rokeby Hall for Thomas Robinson.

14. Between 1768 and 1788 the architect was employed by Henry, 2nd Earl of Darlington, who died in 1792, altering and adding to the fabric of Raby Castle, viz. the entrance hall, the small drawing room, an oval room (now the dining room) and the blue bedroom.

15. The 82' span of Rutherford Bridge was the widest Carr achieved. The note on the drawing reads that it "was built in the year 1773 soon after the other bridge with two arches was taken down by a flood; the whole of this bridge is built with good stone got in the neighbourhood and founded upon a rock the building of which cost the Riding only £400 and raising and making the 100 yards of road at each end thereof cost £100. This bridge was executed by Robert Shout junior of Helmsley according to the plan and directions given by Mr. Carr."

16. Carleton was extensively altered by Carr, c. 1780, for the widow of James Wallace, Attorney-General to George III.

17. Brougham Castle was once owned by Lady Anne Clifford whose grandson sold it to James Bird, only to be disposed of again to John Brougham for £5,000.

18. Hutton John, about a mile from Dacre Castle, was the Hudleston family home, with a castellated pele of the 13th century forming the core of the building.

19. Holker Hall descended via the Lowther family to the Cavendishes. The present L-shaped house is a Victorian rebuild on the site of the early 17th century house built by George Preston. Carr's work of 1783-1789 is in the old wing.

20. Probably Graythwaite Hall at Far Sawrey, a 16th century hall built by the Rawlinsons but altered twice in the 19th century for Colonel Sandys, MP for Bootle.

21. Almost certainly Grizedale Hall at Satterthwaite which was demolished c. 1955.

22. Stoors Hall, overlooking the lake, was built in 1781 for Sir John Legard, the 6th baronet. The Admiral's Temple, a small octagonal tower at the end of a jetty in the lake was built to commemorate English naval victories in the Napoleonic Wars.

23. Fell Foot, Newby Bridge, a 3-storey white stucco, late 18th century house, overlooking Windermere, built by Jeremiah Dixon, Mayor of Leeds in 1784.

24. In the *Universal Directory* for 1794 a Thomas Lever of Tottinton Mill, Blue Boar Court, Manchester is listed as a manufacturer of Muslin, Dimity, etc. There are three cotton manufacturers bearing the same name trading from Abraham's Court, Bolton: Lever & Cartwright, John Lever and William Lever, who also had an address at Lower Ship in Salford, while Hilton Lever worked from Travis' Yard, Bolton. The period between 1788 and 1803 has been called the 'golden age' of the cotton industry, which was revolutionized by the invention of the spinning-jenny, the water-frame and Crompton's mule.

25. Giovanni Battista Guarini, born in Ferrara in 1538, wrote, in 1589, *Il Pastore Fido* in emulation of Tasso's *Arminta*. This work was in vogue in England in the 17th century, when it was translated many times, but most notably by Sir Richard Fanshawe in 1647 as *The Faithful Shepherd*.

26. Kedleston Hall was designed c. 1757 by Matthew Brettingham for Sir Nathaniel Curzon (later 1st Lord Scarsdale), but James Paine built the north front and Robert Adam the south.

27. By 1751 André Planché was making porcelain in Derby, probably at Cockpit Hill. By 1796 William Dewsbury I, an enameller, and John Heath had become the proprietors.

28. Thomas Jarvis (or Jervais) (d. 1799), was born and worked in Dublin with his brother, John, as a glass-painter, and studying the scientific aspects of the trade. He moved to London and in 1777 transferred onto glass Sir Joshua Reynold's designs for the window in New Collage Chapel, Oxford. Besides his work at Lichfield there is also an example at Windsor.

29. By the 1770s Matthew Boulton's Soho factory was an established tourist spot. **Deane & Bridgman** of Moor Street. are the only Birmingham whip makers to come to light so far; whip making was established in the city by 1750, and c. 1780 Matthew Deane of 9, Bull Ring, introduced an "engine", thereby lessening labour and enabling children to be employed in the production of hand whips. **Henry Clay** of New-hall Street is listed in *The Universal Directory* for 1790 as 'Japanner to his Majesty', while *Chambers Dictionary* describes Amelia's 'curious tea boards' as tea trays.

30. *The Universal British Directory* of 1794 lists nine pinmakers for Gloucester; by 1802 eleven firms in the city and in the adjoining parishes were employing 1,500 people, including outworkers, some of whom were from the parish workhouses, who headed and packed the pins. In 1832 Richard Oastler gave evidence to the House of Commons Committee on Child Labour: "… it was the regular custom to work children in factories 13 hours a day, and only allow them half an hour for dinner, and that in many factories they were worked considerably more …"

31. Howard Colvin records that Pearsefield, near Chepstow, Monmouthshire, was rebuilt by Sir John Soane (1757-1693) for George Smith between 1785-1793, while in 1797 Joseph Bonomi (1739-1808) was responsible for the provision of additional wings, including the saloon and staircase, for Sir Mark Wood, Bart.

32. Celia Fiennes writes: '… I went 2 miles to the hott spring of water which lookes exceeding cleer and is as warm as new milk and much of that sweetness; this is just by St. Vincents Rocks …'

33. A father and son, both named John Wood, were largely responsible for the creation of 18th century Bath; the Assembly Room was built in 1728, extended in 1750 and the Upper Rooms added in 1771; work began on Queen Square in 1729, the Pump Room was enlarged in 1751 and rebuilt in 1780, while Gay Street dates from 1760 and the Circus from 1766. Ralph Allen (1694-1794), Alexander Pope's 'Man of Bath' was not only involved in rebuilding the city, but for providing the stone required from his quarries.

34. In 1568 Robert Smythson commenced work on the present house at Longleat for John Thynne, Marquis of Bath. Later, the grounds were landscaped by 'Capability' Brown.

35. The Palladian house at Stourhead was built by Colen Campbell in 1723 for Henry Hoare, the banker. Henry Hoare II spent 40 years turning the grounds into an Arcadian landscape, including many of the features found at Studley Royal. In 1791 his successor, Sir Richard Colt Hoare introduced the first rhododendron. (See Harriet's Diary for 1795).

36. The 50-foot high Tower was built in 1772 by Henry Flitcroft.

37. Alderman Beckford, who died in 1770, left his 9-year old son, William, a huge country house, an estate to match, £1.5 million in capital and an income of £70,000 which derived from plantations in Jamaica. In 1787 Sir John Soane was the architect of the picture gallery at Fonthill House, but this was destroyed when a new house was built by William, by now an eccentric, aesthetic collector; it was known as Fonthill Splendens.

38. Salisbury Cathedral was built between 1220 and 1280, with the 404-foot spire, the tallest in England, being added in 1334.

39. Wilton stands on the site of an Abbey founded by Alfred the Great; the first house was destroyed by fire in 1647 and was rebuilt by Inigo Jones.

40. Was 'Mr Cox' actually Dr William Coxe for whom Sir Joan Soane submitted designs for alterations to Bemerton Rectory in Wiltshire? Bemerton is on the road from Wilton to Salisbury. 'Mr Lethulier' was probably a member of the Lethieullier family who were donors of materials of scientific interest to the British Museum, and descended from Sir John Lethieullier, Sheriff of London in 1674, of Aldersbrook Manor House, Little Ilford, Essex.

41. Basildon Park, set in 400 acres, was built by John Carr between 1776 and 1783; there is delicate plasterwork, an elegant staircase, an octagonal drawing room and a shell room.

42. Fawley Court, Henley-on-Thames was designed and built by Sir Christopher Wren for Colonel W. Freeman; it was decorated by Grinling Gibbons and by James Wyatt.

43. Field-Marshall Henry Seymour Conway, M.P. and Governor and Captain of Jersey (1719-1795) was a hero of the Seven Years' War. When he retired from Parliament he spent all his time at Park House in Henley, propogating poplar trees from a cutting brought from Lombardy by Lord Rochford. His daughter was Mrs. Dormer who statue of the King the girls had seen in Edinburgh. The house was altered c. 1796 by Henry Holland (1745-1806).

44. Dr. Richard Robinson (1709-1794), Lord Primate of Ireland, became 1st Baron Rokeby in the peerage of Ireland; he was the sixth son of William Robinson (1675-1720) of Rokeby and brother of Sir Thomas Robinson, 1st Baronet of Rokeby (?1700-1777). Dr. William Markham (1719-1807) was Archbishop of York from 1777; his portrait was painted by Reynolds in 1760.

45. Blenheim Palace, the nation's gift to the Duke of Marlborough, was designed by Sir John Vanbrugh and built between 1705 and 1722. Henry Wise designed the first garden but it was 'Capability' Brown who landscaped the grounds to provide the lake.

46. The manor house of West Hillingdon was rebuilt in 1717 by Meinhard, Duke of Leinster and 3rd Duke of Schomberg, who was with William of Orange at the Battle of the Boyne. It was destroyed by fire in 1844 and replaced by the present building.

47. The Panorama or *Eidophusikon* was a 'moving panorama peep-show' invented by the artist J.P. De Loutherbourg in 1782; he showed views in and about London at different times of the day. Gainsborough and Reynolds were frequent visitors to Panton Square where it was exhibited, and Reynolds is said to have recommended "the ladies in his extensive circle to take their daughters who cultivated drawing, as the best school to witness the power of nature ... "

48. Lever's Museum in Leicester Square housed a natural history collection; it was also known as the *Holophusikon.*

49. In 1770 Philip Astley (1742-1814), a theatrical manager and equestrian, opened a circus at Lambeth. *Astley's Amphitheatre* was built in the 1790s on Westminster Bridge Road, and was a music hall-cum-hippodrome, with a stage, an orchestra and, as the name suggests, horses. In Harriet's Diary she mentions that in the Amphitheatre in Edinburgh, which held 1,500, "the Equestrian exploits, dancing and tumbling are the same as Astleys in London." It is also mentioned by Charles Dickens in *The Old Curiosity Shop.*

50. Newark Town Hall and Assembly Rooms date from 1773-1776. It seems that the building of the left-hand wing of the Town Hall was delayed because the lease of a public house on the site, *The Green Dragon*, still had not expired. Changing its name to *The Wing Tavern*, the pub moved across the Market Place where, according to Rodney Cousins in *Newark Inns and Public Houses*, it began trading in 1775 and continues to the present day.

Amelia Clark's Journal
through North Wales from Thorp Arch
made in the year 1798

6th August   On the 6th of August we set out from Thorp Arch and arrived at Wakefield at my Uncle Carr's to dinner where we spent three pleasant days and from thence we went to Halifax and spent the evening at Mr. Waterhouse's[1] very pleasantly. Two of the Misses Waterhouse play charmingly on the harpsichord and Organ. The Country round Halifax is extremely bold and beautiful and the Road from thence to Oldham, lately made along the Caldervale, is extremely picturesque, and much less mountaineous than going over Blackstone edge. We dined at Oldham, & from thence we went to Rochdale and Littleborough, where my Uncle changed one of his horses which had fall'n lame.

7th August   The next day we went to see Lord Grey de Wilton's house[2] which is a modern building, the inside of which is beautifully finish'd by Mr. Wyatt[3], and there are some pretty modern paintings, and Arabesque ornaments, done by Rebecca[4] (in her Ladyship's dressing room).

   We next proceeded to Manchester where I visited several young Ladies of my acquaintance, & from thence we went to Moor Town. The next day we breakfasted at Northwich, & proceeded over the Forest of Delamere to Chester. Beeston Castle has a noble appearance on the road, the Country round which is exceeding flat and inanimate. Chester is a very singular built Town and is surrounded by a wall and a walk round it like York. On each side of several streets there are paved areas, where everybody walks, raised about 10 feet above the level of the pavement, & which they call the Rows; on one side are shops and on the other the chamber story of each house which projects over the Rows is supported towards the street by Columns. One therefore walks perfectly dry in these rows in bad weather.

   On Sunday morning we went to Church at the great Cathedral, which is an Antient Gothick building, the outside of which is very much decay'd. Here we met with young Mr. and Mrs. Peterson who walked round the City with us, and with whom we spent the Evening.

   The next day we set out for Wales, and slept the first night at Hawarden in Flintshire. This County is bounded by an arm of the Irish sea, which forms the great Estuary of the river Dee on the North side, and Denbighshire on the South, and is the least of all the Countys in Wales. It abounds with Coal & Lead mines, and the views from Halkin

Old House in Watergate Street, Chester

Alfred Summers delt

W. Banks sc [&c]

high hills of the Irish sea & of the Rivers Dee and Mersey, and the town of Liverpool, are magnificently grand and extensive. The County town of Flint stands on the Banks of the River Dee, and is a small town govern'd by a Mayor and Burgesses. Here is the ruins of a Castle built by Edward I; the assizes are held here.

From Halkin we went through Northop to Holywell, which is near the market town of Caerwys; at this place we breakfasted, and was attended with the Music of a Welsh harper, after which we visited the celebrated spring call'd St. Winefride's Well, to which the monkish writers ascribe many miraculous Cures by bathing in it. A very beautiful Gothick building still remains over the Well which was erected in Henry VII's time, over which is a Chapel. We were told that the spring issues one hundred tons of water every minute. Two Cotton mills and a Corn mill are turned by the stream, which runs into the Sea at about two miles distant through a beautifully wooded Ravine.

We next proceeded towards St. Asaph over Heath hill, from which place we had a Grand view of the magnificent Vale of Clwyd; the small City of St. Asaph stands in this vale, near which are two rivers, the Clwyd and the Elwy. The Cathedral is a very plain building. Dr. Shirley is the Bishop, and there is a Dean, Six prebendaries, seven Canons, four Vicars choral, an Organist, four singing men and four boys.

At a little distance from St. Asaph we had a fine view of Rhuddland Castle built by Llewellyn ap Sitsyll, prince of Wales.[5] At this place King Edward II with all his court frequently spent their Christmas holidays.

In the afternoon we reach'd the pretty little Town call'd Abbergelle, about a mile from the Sea where there are very fine Sands of a vast extent, and a great deal of company come here to Bath in the Sea. The Inns were full of company from the neighbourhood of Manchester.

Our next stage from this place was to Aberconway which, with its beautiful Castle and its surrounding walls and towers, is built upon an Elevated Rock, upon the margin of the noble River Conway. The whole of these fortifications and Castle were built by Edward I, the appearance of which from the ferry house, with the adjoining hanging woods and the noble river in the foreground, compose one of the most grand and picturesque views I ever beheld.

We cross'd the River with our carriage, horses, & other passengers in a large vessel at about twelve miles distance from the Sea, and from Conway we proceeded on the road towards the City of Bangor, in the way to which place we were surprised by the steep and dangerous descent of the road down a mountain call'd Pen Maen Bach, the declivity of which, and the deep Glen on one side of the road, was horrible. At the bottom of this mountain we crossed a small rivulet on a level with the sea which appear'd betwixt the mountains through a narrow valley; from this valley we began to ascend again by a narrow winding road, along the side of an Enormous mountain call'd Pen Maen Mawr, which is covered with Gigantic Rocks scattered in Chaotick confusion, through which a narrow road is cut; this overhangs the Roaring sea two hundred & fifty yards immediately below you on one side of the road, & on the other there are tremendous huge broken rocks, forming a scene so sublimely Grand & terrific to the astonish'd Eye, as to fill the mind with reverential awe and admiration.[6]

The next place which attracted our notice was Ld. Pennant's house, near Llandegai[7]; the house is a handsome Gothick building, and from which is a beautiful view towards the Church, the new bridge, and the River, which runs through the valley near the house, the approach to which is through a Gothick Gateway, a little way beyond which there is a charming view of the Town of Beaumaris, the Peris mountain and the Isle of Anglesea across the Menay Strait[8], which runs through a charming Valley towards the City of Bangor, the Country round which place is very beautiful. The Cathedral is a very plain structure dedicated to St. Dienal; besides the Bishop there is a Dean, Archdeacon, two prebendaries, two Vicars choral, a precentor and an Organist. Here we spent the Evening at a good Inn. At Supper we had very good fish, Mullet it was call'd.

In the morning we proceeded to Caernarvon along a beautiful Road, with the Irish Sea on the west side of us and separated by the Menay Strait from the Isle of Anglesea and on the East side of the road rise in Majestic grandeur the Snowdon Hills to an amazing height, which are so call'd from their being covered with snow one half of the year, in the Center of which above all the others, the Celebrated Snowdon rises, which is call'd in Welsh, Clogwyn Carnedd y Wyddfa.[9] From the top of this hill may be seen part of England, Scotland, Ireland and the Isle of Man. This mountain has not, however, so interesting an appearance from its irregular form as Skiddaw or Helvellyn in Cumberland.

On our arrival at Caernarvon we found great difficulty to get accommodations, as it was the time of the assizes. The beautiful and singular appearance of the Castle first attracted our notice, and it is a noble specimen of antient military architecture, built by Edward I to curb the Welsh mountaineers, and to secure a passage to the Isle of Anglesea. It is situated at the South end of the noble Menay Strait; the entrance into the Castle is through a lofty Gateway under a stupendous Tower, in the front of which appears a Gigantic statue of the Conqueror, grasping in his right hand a dagger. The several Polygonal towers are very beautiful and are crown'd with Elegant Turrets & Embrasures. We were shewn the room where the first Prince of Wales was born, which is a decagon of about 33 feet diameter as each side thereof is nine feet six inches. The whole town has been fortified, and on walking on the Ramparts by the sea side my Uncle was accosted by Judge Sutton and Councillor Brough of Newark.[10] On conversing with them, they advised us to go and see the Romantic scenery of Pont Aber Glaslyn, or the Devil's Work, as the country people call it, which is about 14 miles from Caernarvon. After dinner we set out, and the road to the place winds round the foot of Snowdon. On our approach nearer the place, we entered into a deep narrow Valley, formed betwixt two immense mountains of Rocks, which by degrees contracted our narrow broken road close to the Edge of a Rapid River rolling over broken Rocks until we came to the Pont, or Bridge, at the bottom of this dismal Glen. At this Spot the view is particularly interesting; the River appears at our feet, dashing and Roaring through a bed of huge misshapen Rocks, and forming in its struggle numberless whirlpools, Eddies and small Cascades, through which we saw the Salmon leaping & struggling through the Cascades and Rocks. We crossed the bridge into Merionethshire and ascended a mountain, from whence we had a View of the beautiful Lake below us.

We return'd from this singular scenery by Moonlight, along the banks of a charming, transparent Lake near the foot of Snowdon, near which we saw also two beautiful Cascades. On our arrival at Caernarvon we went to the new Hotel where we were comfortably accommodated.

The next morning we cross'd the Menay Strait near the Castle and ascended by a pretty road to the summit of a mountain & a Summer house, from which we had a very extensive View across the Bay of Caernavon, over the Isle of Anglesea and the Snowdon mountains; in returning to our Hotel we passed by the Plas Mawr or Great House which was once perhaps the residence of the Lord of the Manor; by the conspicuous date it was built in 1691 and is a good specimen of the awkward side of architecture of that time, which is neither Gothick nor Classical, but an heterogeneous mixture of both.

From this charming place we return'd again to Bangor where there is a comfortable Inn, and the next day we crossed over the dreadful Pen Maen Mawr again to Aberconway where, in the Churchyard, there is a Tomb stone with the following very extraordinary inscription:

> *Here lieth the body of Nicholas Hook, Gent.*
> *who was the one & fortieth child of his Father*
> *Willm. Hook Esq. by Alice his Wife,*
> *and the Father of 27 Children.*
> *He died the 20th day of March 1637.*

Mill on the Llanberris side of Snowdon

We cross'd the Ferry and spent our Evening at Mrs. Davies's of the Ferry house near Conway, and the next morning we proceeded to Abergele to breakfast, and from thence we went very near St. Asaph again, in order to go through the noble Vale of Clwyd to Denbigh, where we dined and spent the afternoon in viewing the extensive remains of the Castle built by Edward I, which is situated upon a Rock. This is call'd by the Welsh Lledvyrnyn Rhos, or Rocky Hill, from which we had a delightful prospect over the Rich and extensive Vale of Clwyd.

A part of the noble Gateway & entrance into the Castle is still standing, the walls of which are 14 feet thick; over the Entrance is a Rude Statue of Edward, the founder. The vestiges of the great Room in which that Prince entertain'd the Welsh Knights is very visible, and appears to be near 200 feet in length and 50 feet in width. This Town is chiefly inhabited by Glovers and Tanners and is govern'd by a Recorder, Two Aldermen and two Bailiffs, and they have a decent Town hall.

At Llansannan, a little way from Denbigh, is a Cave Cut out of the side of a great Rock, which contains twentyfour seats and is known by the name of King Arthur's round Table.[11]

The next morning we proceeded along the beautiful Vale of Clwyd to Ruthin, which is a pretty Town, & situated in the Center of the Vale, near which are several Druidical remains and Stone Chests. From Ruthin we went to Wrexham where we dined and went afterwards to the Church, it being Sunday. The inside of the Church is very handsome & capacious and there is a noble Organ very whimsically play'd by a blind Man, with light quirks of Music broken and uneven "to make the soul dance upon a Jig to Heaven", as Pope said of Handel when he heard him play at the Duke of Chandos' Chapel. The tower adjoining this Church is very high, and is one of the most beautiful Gothick structures I ever beheld. Wrexham is a large Town and well built and has a great market for the sale of Flannels which are manufactured in this County.

From this Town we proceeded by a very good road to Chester, where we again visited Mr. and Mrs. Peterson and Miss Peterson. We visited also the new Prison and Courts of Justice design'd by Mr. Harrison[12], which my Uncle thought were very handsome and convenient.

We now bid adieu to North Wales, the Tour through which has afforded us the highest pleasure - whether we Contemplate the Romantic and magnificent scenes of nature with which the Country abounds, Or the natural Civility & obliging manners of the Inhabitants at every place we passed through. The women in general have very good complexions and they dress exactly alike. They wear a pettycoat of

Tabley House

either Blue or striped Flannel, a Kind of Bedgown of the same stuff, of a Brown striped Colour, a Broad handkerchief over the neck and shoulders, a neat Mob Cap and a Man's hat; in cold and bad weather they wear a long blue Cloak which descends below the Knee; when they are not particularly dressed they often go without shoes or stockings.

The Man's dress is a Jacket, Waistcoat and Breeches of their Country Flannel, the stockings, which the Men always wear, are tied under the Knee with Red Garters. They are naturally vivacious and Cheerful, not exhibiting that appearance of Torpor and dejection which appear in the labouring poor of our own Country; their wants, being few, are easily supplied, a little milk from their own Mountain Goats, an Oaten Cake and Potatoes furnish the only meal which they desire. Confined to their own mountains, they see no scenes of profusion to excite envy or discontent by a comparison between their own penury and the abundance of others.

From Chester we proceeded over the Forest of Delamere towards Northwich; at a little distance Beeston Castle has a Majestic appearance from its elevated situation in this flat Country. From Northwich we visited Sir John Leicester's noble house[13], designed by my Uncle Carr, in which there are a good many fine paintings, and one room is adorn'd with Arabesque paintings and Ornament copied from the Vatican at Rome. In the Center of the Front of this house is a noble Portico of Columns in one stone, each of which is 30 feet in height.

From this place we went to Knutsford in Cheshire, where we spent the Evening, and the next day we breakfasted at Macclesfield, which is a large town, full of Cotton manufacturers, and from thence we travell'd over very mountainous, Romantic Country to Buxton, where we spent a week very pleasantly. The place was never known so full of company, which made the Ball nights very splendid & agreeable.

We next Visited the noble palace of Chatsworth where we spent many pleasant days, in the way to which place we pass'd through the Grand Ravine call'd Middleton dale [a description of which is mention'd in a former Tour, near the beginning of this book]. From Chatsworth we went to Wentworth house where I staid a considerable time. From this noble place we went to my Uncle's house at new Lodge, near Barnsley, where we staid two Months in visiting and receiving the Visits of our Relations and friends in that pleasant neighbourhood.

We next went to my Uncle Carr's at Wakefield where we spent a fortnight very agreeably, and from which place we return'd to Thorp Arch[14] again on the 17th of November, having been absent from thence very near four Months.

Footnotes - 1798

1. Well Head House, near Halifax, built by John Carr c. 1770 for John Waterhouse. Demolished 1971.

2. Heaton Hall, near Oldham, Lancashire, built by James Wyatt in 1772; formerly the residence of the Earls of Wilton.

3. James Wyatt (1746-1813). After spending six years in Italy Wyatt built the neo-classical Pantheon in London (1772). Besides building in the neo-classical style he also became a leading figure in the Gothic Revival.

4. Biagio Rebecca (1735-1808): of Italian descent, but lived and worked in England; specialised in imitation of antique bas-relief. Heaton Hall contains one of the few surviving Etruscan rooms, with painted walls and ceiling. Also worked at Audley End, Harewood, Kedleston, Somerset House and Windsor Castle. Became an ARA in 1771.

5. Rhuddlan had two castles; the original is believed to have been sited on Twt Hill, less than a quarter of a mile from the one built by Edward I in 1277-82. The original was built in the eleventh century by Llewellyn ap Sitsyll or Seisyllt. Amelia spells all the Welsh names phonetically.

6. It has been said that "when the wind hurls in from the sea the passage westward is an experience to be remembered." Thomas Macaulay (1800-1859), the essayist, wrote: "The great route through Wales to Holyhead was in such a state in 1685 that a viceroy, going to Ireland, was five hours in travelling fourteen miles, from St. Asaph to Conway. Between Conway and Beaumaris he was forced to walk a great part of the way; and his lady was carried in a litter. His coach was, with great difficulty, and by the help of many hands, brought after him entire. In general, carriages were taken to pieces at Conway and borne on the shoulders of stout Welsh peasants to the Menai Straits."

7. Amelia wrote of 'Ld. Pynsent's house near Landy Quy'. It was. in fact, Penrhyn Castle, at Llandegai, the seat of Richard Pennant, who was created Baron Penrhyn in the peerage of Ireland in 1783. His income came from inherited Jamaican sugar plantations and from slate quarries he developed in the nearby Nant Ffrancon valley.

8. Amelia mistakenly believes the Menai Strait to be a river.

9. In the Diary the names were recorded phonetically as Klogwyn Karneadh y Wyddva - there is no letter 'K' in the Welsh alphabet.

10. According to the Universal Directory for 1794 Job Brough was Town Clerk of Newark; his name also appears under "Brough & Godfrey, Attorneys."

    Newark was represented by two burgesses in Parliament, and in 1791 a Mr. Sutton and a Mr. Crosbie, for the 'Blues' or democrats, were returned.

11. The Cefn Rocks, some 2½ miles from St. Asaph.

12. Thomas Harrison (1744-1829). Among other buildings also designed, in the Classical style, the Portico Library, Manchester, which opened in 1806.

13. Tabley Hall, built by John Carr between 1762-9 for Sir Peter Leicester Bt. together with the stables and gate lodges.

14. Thorp Arch Hall was built by Carr for William Gossip of York between 1750 and 1754.

Bibliography

Alsopp, B., and Ursula Clark,
*Historic Architecture of Northumberland &
Newcastle-upon-Tyne*
Oriel Press, Stockefield,
Northumberland, 1977

Beard, G.,
The Greater House in Cumbria
Westmorland Gazette, Kendal, 1978

Burke, B.,
Dictionary of Landed Gentry
Harrison, London, 1858

Burke's Peerage and Baronetage
Burke's Peerage Limited, London, 1909

Clark, C.F.G.,
*The Genealogy of the Family of the
"Clarks", of Bankside House Thorne, near
Doncaster, and laterly of Ellinthorp Hall,
near Boroughbridge, Yorkshire.*
Browesholme Papers, Lancashire
Record Office, reference DDB acc
6685, Box 111, bundle 1.

Colvin, Howard,
*A Biographical Dictionary of British
Architects, 1660-1840*
Yale University Press, London and
New York, 1995, 3rd edition.

Forsyth, R.O.,
The Beauties of Scotland
Thomson Bonar & John Brown,
Edinburgh, 1805. 6 volumes.

Graham, F.,
*The Old Halls, Houses and Inns of
Northumberland*
F. Graham, Newcastle-upon-Tyne,
1977

Hatcher, J.,
Richmondshire Architecture
C.J. Hatcher, Richmond, Yorks., 1990.

Liddington, J.,
Anne Lister of Halifax
Rivers Oram Press, London & New
York, 1998

Morris, C., (Editor),
The Journeys of Celia Fiennes
Cresset Press, London, 1947

Oastler, Richard
in: Alasdair Clayre (Editor),
Nature & Industrialization
Oxford University Press, Oxford, 1977

Osborne, H., (Editor),
Oxford Companion to Art
Oxford University Press, Oxford, 1981
edition

Parry, Melanie (Editor)
Chamber's Biographical Dictionary
Chambers Harrop Publishers Ltd.,
Edinburgh 1997

Robinson, J.M.,
*A Guide to the Country Houses of the
North West*
Constable, London, 1988

Room, A. (Revised by)
Brewer's Dictionary of Phrase and Fable
Cassell, London, 1999

Stephen, Sir Leslie, & Sidney Lee (Editors)
Dictionary of National Biography
Oxford University Press, London, 1917

Universal British Directory
Vol. 1 (1790), Vol. 2 (1793), A-D;
Vol. 3 (1794), E-M; Vol. 4 (1798),
N-Z; Vol. 5, Appendix and
Supplements.
Wakefield E.P. Publishers, 1980

Waterson, E., & P. Meadows,
Lost Houses of the West Riding
Jill Raines, 1998

Waterson, E., & P. Meadows,
Lost Houses of York and the North Riding
Jill Raines, 1998

Whitaker, N.,
*The Old Halls and Manor Houses of
Durham*
Frank Graham, Newcastle-upon-Tyne,
1975

Worsley, G.,
*John Carr's Last Tour - A Romantic
Excursion of 1805*
Country Life, pp. 132-133, April 10,
1987

Worsley, G.,
Crediting Carr
Country Life, pp. 162-165, May 5,
1988

York Georgian Society
The Works in Architecture of John Carr
Sessions of York, 1973

Youngson, A.J.,
The Making of Classical Edinburgh
University Press, Edinburgh, 1988